DON'T FORGET

the

Angels

Dedication

To my dear wife, Sue, and our three children, Lucy, Tom, and Abbie. I think you are all amazing.

Acknowledgments

Thank you to everyone who has taken time to share their angel stories with me. I have included some of these in this book.

Thank you to my wife, Sue, and our children, Lucy, Tom, and Abbie, for allowing me to share some of your stories. You all constantly challenge me to live off the map as we have together made so many discoveries in God.

Thank you to Tony and Margaret Howson for your constant support and encouragement over many years and for your unusual ability to break down the walls and embrace fresh pastures.

Thank you to Duncan and Kate Smith, few would open their lives as you have. I love your wholehearted pursuit after the things of the Kingdom.

Thank you to my many friends at The Community Church; it's been an amazing privilege to run the race with you.

Thank you to Pietro Evangelista and the team at Destiny Image Europe for helping make this book a reality.

Above all, I am so grateful to God for everything—life is so much fun with You.

Endorsements

Nick Pengelly answers the cry of your heart for more of God's supernatural. This timely book is full of thrilling stories of angelic interventions and the role and function of angels in everyday life. It provides fresh revelation about the ministry of angels and how we can cooperate with them to see Heaven come to earth. I found the book to be very engaging because of Nick's amazing insights into the supernatural realm of the Spirit and the way he gives an accurate biblical picture of the spiritual world. I highly recommend this book with all my heart.

Gary Oates
Author, "Open My Eyes, Lord"
International Conference Speaker

There is a new interest among believers in the ministry of angels. Nick Pengelly has written *Don't Forget the Angels* as a guide for those experiencing this new desire. In a very readable book, Nick gives an excellent overview of the biblical material regarding angels and intersperses it with great stories and personal experiences. I found the chapter, Guest for Dinner, to be very challenging. Nick shares about "entertaining angels without knowing it"—how easy it is not to respond at inconvenient times to someone in need. That someone may be an angel sent to minister to us in a special way! I think believers will find *Don't Forget the Angels* informative, enjoyable, and encouraging.

Rev. Barry Manuel
Senior Pastor, Morphett Vale Baptist Church
Adelaide, South Australia

Nick Pengelly is an apostolic man with a hunger for the prophetic and supernatural. As a friend, I fully believe in his ministry and vision. As a fellow minister, I believe in his ministry to the nations as it brings about healing, church planting, and the spirit of revival.

Todd Bentley
Revivalist
FreshFire Ministries

Contents

Foreword

I was incredibly excited as I listened to my spiritual father and Pastor, John Arnott, founding Pastor of Toronto Airport Christian Fellowship. He was preaching about the power of prophetic symbolism, and I realized that throughout the Old Testament men and women encountered angels, spoke with them conversationally, and had incredible supernatural dreams, visions, and visitations–yet they were under the old covenant.

My heart started racing as I thought about the significance of this fact. If this was true of them, then how much more should it be our experience now that we have been brought into the new covenant in Christ–now that we are God's children and filled with His Spirit! First Corinthians 6: 17 says that, *"He who is joined to the Lord is one spirit with Him."* We should regularly experience the angels and live in the realm of the supernatural–that's our home in Christ Jesus!

Growing up in Africa in a strongly evangelical missionary family I was led to believe that talking with angels was not to be done. But I came to realize that this belief was wrong, very wrong. The Scriptures are overflowing with lengthy conversations between men and angels. We'd have to scrap much of Ezekiel, Zechariah, Revelation, and half of Daniel.

I began to open my heart and ask God to teach me about the supernatural. Within two months I met Nick Pengelly while ministering at his incredible church in Wrexham, North Wales. He has since become a beloved friend—the Lord instantly joined our hearts as I fired supernatural arrows and bombs at him and he did so in return.

During a trip to Kyrgyzstan I asked Nick to pray for me and teach me about the angels and the supernatural realm. I remember the eyes of my heart opening as I listened to him and prepared for the meeting that evening when I would be preaching.

Approximately 800 Kyrgyz people filled the church. I invited the angels like Nick encouraged me to and bang! Heaven fell on the place. As I spoke, the Holy Spirit fell, the angels came, and spontaneous healings and miracles exploded throughout. All 800 people received immediate deliverance as the demonic was driven out of them in the presence of God. Since then, I share Nick's parting words to me with everyone I meet, *"Don't forget the angels."* Whenever I invite the angels, there is transformation.

Friends, I encourage you with all my heart to read this awesome book. Let it sink right in. Pause and pray, asking your Heavenly Daddy to open your eyes, and then give yourself permission to go on a journey into His supernatural Kingdom of love. You will begin to partner with His angels as you live and work by the Spirit, from your life in Christ. Have fun and *Don't forget the angels!*

Duncan Smith
Executive Director of Catch the Fire Ministries
Youth and Young Adult Network Lead Pastors
Toronto Airport Christian Fellowship

Chapter 1

EYES THAT SEE

The Scriptures are full of amazing supernatural events, moments when God in His sovereignty intervenes. There are many accounts of angels turning up, bringing messages, opening prison doors, and appearing in dreams and visions. There are awesome signs where massive rivers part, fire comes from Heaven, buildings shake, and the sun stands still. During the wilderness times of the Old Testament year after year God miraculously feeds His people with strange food from Heaven. The response of the people to their new food is very similar to our reaction today to the supernatural and signs and wonders. They asked, "What is it?" Exodus 16:14-15 says:

> *When the dew was gone, thin flakes like frost on the ground appeared on the desert floor. When the Israelites saw it, they said to each other, "What is it?" For they did not know what it was. Moses said to them, "It is the bread the Lord has given you to eat."*

Moses was already carrying the revelation from God about this amazing sign. He was able to tell the people what it was and how they should respond. Today we are in times when the supernatural realms are opening up to every believer in a fresh way. If we are going to live in the fullness of His Kingdom there will be many times when we will think, "What is it?"

The Israelites had to eat the manna to live. If we are going to live in all that God has to give us in these days, we are going to have to fully open our hearts to major heaven-initiated events, this will include angelic visitations, open heavens, and signs and wonders. The fact that you have picked up this book suggests that there is something in your heart that desires to know more about the angelic and the supernatural realms of God. My objective is to help open believer's eyes to angels and the heavenly realms. We can all engage in supernatural experiences having a confidence that comes from a strong scriptural basis.

At the same time we must recognize that God initiates these moments. In day to day life I am aware that I can easily miss obvious things around me because I do not pay attention. The same applies to the angelic realm. Even if we train our senses in these realms there will be times when angels come in human form, can even eat with us, and we are unaware! I wonder what dinner conversation would be like with these heaven-sent visitors.

Every Journey Has a Beginning

I have always had a strong desire to find out about spiritual things. When I first became a Christian over 20 years ago I was fascinated by speaking in tongues, spiritual gifts, and signs and wonders. It was not long before I was responding to the word in Corinthians that tells us to eagerly desire spiritual gifts, especially the gift of prophecy. I started desperately praying that God would use me to prophesy. At that time it appeared that the way into these supernatural things was like trying to find a secret hideaway. The access through the hidden doorway was only open to some special Christians. I followed the vague thought that I might become holy enough, have prayed sufficiently, or have read enough of the Bible, to be given the directions to the hidden place. My best hope seemed to be that I would see everything more clearly when I died. As I look back I know that God did not make things that way.

Since those days of youthful pursuit I have continued to ask God to uncover the supernatural. I have regularly experienced the gifts of the Spirit. I have seen where prophets have brought accurate prophetic words about people's destinies as well as bringing people hope, healing, and comfort. For many years I would attend each meeting hoping that God would give me a prophetic word to speak out. I placed a lot of pressure on myself and ended up thinking that I had not been good enough for Him to speak through.

These times reminded me of the crippled man who had spent years waiting by the water for an angel to come and stir the waters. Even when the waters did stir he was not quite in the right place and some-one else got into the waters first and he missed out! One day Jesus came to him and basically said, you don't have to wait—there is another way. Jesus commanded him to get up, pick up his mat, and walk.

For me, a prophet was visiting the local church, she prophesied over people in great detail. She had accurate words over dozens of people she had never met. I realized there was a different way, God was willing to talk at any time and in any place. My faith increased considerably and I found there was a daily prophetic flow available for me to step into. This flow is available for each of us.

Since then I have experienced the healing power of God, known times when healing did not come easily, and searched deep in my heart when healings eluded me. In my heart I knew there was so much more that God wanted me to embrace. The depths of the Scriptures pointed to many things that were not within my Christian experiences. The events that happened to the adventurers of faith in the Bible stayed within the confines of Scripture. The angelic realms were one of these mysterious areas. It seemed easier and felt safer to stay within the boundaries of the things I knew, but at the same time I knew that I needed to go off the map of my limited experience.

Taste and See

Our history (especially church history), our life experience, and maybe some negative memories can be major limiting factors in our journey with God. My natural personality is to be cautious. I have to constantly break through caution to engage my faith in the supernatural realm. My children provided me a good example of how we can easily reject something that is good, simply because it is outside our norm.

One of my hobbies is growing vegetables. I particularly enjoy growing unusual and unfamiliar varieties of everyday crops. A bowl of black and white or pink tomatoes, golden beetroot, radishes that have the heat of chilis, and pumpkins like carriages are among the novelties that have made good discussion topics. A couple of years ago I grew an extremely unusual variety of potato called Salad Blue. This is an old variety of potato that would have appeared on the Victorian aristocracy's dinner table.

The tubers did not have the expected yellowy, white flesh. When you cut them in half they revealed deep purple color all the way through. I was delighted when I found they made spectacular mashed potato and none of the purple color was lost in the cooking process. They looked like I had added a generous portion of food coloring. My children, who normally enjoy an adventure, arrived at the meal table and looked wide-eyed at the unfamiliar offering on their plates. It was obvious that they were not going to eat any of "that stuff" amid noisy exclamations, "What is it?!"

Before I could react, purple potato was flying at me from three directions. I soon had a very large mound on my plate. Slightly disappointed at their reaction I was determined to enjoy the normal taste of creamy mashed potato but I struggled to finish my super-sized meal. Just think, the varieties that we consider strange and unfamiliar today were considered normal to previous generations. But their uniqueness has been lost in the commercial drive for productivity and uniformity. It is easy to become comfortable with the status quo and reject and judge everything else.

If we are going to grow and learn about the supernatural realms we need to examine things that are unfamiliar. We cannot afford to reject them without looking. We need to take the time to examine things in light of Scripture. I am glad that over the years God has brought many people across my path who have encouraged me to think differently. It has been a process, and I constantly renew my thinking. Allowing my mind to be transformed by the things of the

Kingdom of God, often the very things I first rejected, were the things I later repented over and accepted. By His grace God has worked through any hardness of heart, so that fresh pastures are experienced.

A Spiritual Hunger

There seems to be a major fascination with all types of spiritual things. The attraction to spiritual things is not limited to Christians. A quick look through newspapers, television programs, and local events indicate people's desire to connect with a spiritual world. There are many people who avidly read their horoscopes, go to psychics, or watch supernatural events on the television. We need to remember that anything God has available for us in the Spirit, the enemy will have ways of imitating.

God has released the gift of prophecy through the Holy Spirit as a valid way of speaking to His people. He can reveal many things in people's hearts with the purpose of building them up and drawing them closer to Himself. Even the lives of people who do not believe that God exists can be dramatically changed by these encounters with God. I have seen evangelists used by God to bring words of knowledge that speak right into the heart of people and result in their salvation. When satan reveals things through physics and clairvoyants, they may be accurate in some ways but he aims to confuse people and leave them further away from the Heavenly Father.

As believers we can easily shy away from the supernatural out of a fear that we will somehow be led astray. But there is nothing in Scripture to say that these realms are not available for us today. It is worth spending some time looking through the Scriptures and reading about supernatural events, healing, and visitations of angels. The Book of Acts is full of them; they were a mark of the New Testament Church. What an amazing thing to realize—there is so much more to see than what we see with our natural eyes and God wants to show us while we are alive on earth. In John's gospel Jesus says that those who are born again will see the Kingdom (see John 3:3). This is a sight I desire and something I believe God makes available to the whole Body of Christ.

The purpose of this book is to share some of my journey. The journey is still in its infancy and continues to be an exciting voyage of discovery. I will take some time to examine the purposes of God revealed in creation and throughout Scriptures. I will share my experiences as I have pressed forward on the adventure.

One thing I quickly discovered was that we need to be with others who are walking the same way. The Body of Christ is not made to be separated or in isolation from each other. We need one another to grow quickly in the fullness of the Kingdom. If we try and stand alone we can easily go off track. We also need to apply the basic principles of a Godly life. In another chapter you will see how applying basic principles in our lives releases angelic activity as well as closes the door to demonic interference. I have also explained the personal effect of angelic intervention—having had the privilege to witness those who have a clear seer anointing.

There have been many times when I have felt that there was angelic activity taking place, both in church gatherings, during daily life, and even in the region around. I have regularly asked questions of the seers and they have been able to confirm and establish what was taking place. These experiences have caused my faith to increase and helped me learn to partner with the angelic realm. I believe that the clearer our vision becomes in the heavenly realms the more we become like Jesus, who only did what He saw His Father doing.

Welcoming Angels

It is time for us to welcome angelic activity into our lives and our church gatherings. Jesus told his disciples that the Kingdom belongs to children, and we have to be like them to enter in. I have found that children often have amazing abilities to see the activities of angels. Later in the book I recount some of their stories. They will capture your heart and provoke you to seek God for a greater awareness of heavenly realms.

As you read, enjoy the journey, embrace the adventure. This is a road that can only be walked in faith. As I have moved on I have found that God is more exciting and adventurous than I ever dared to believe. He often takes me far from my comfort zones. This is where faith grows; this is the realm of signs, wonders, healings, and deliverance. Angels are often closely involved. We have to see through the eyes of our hearts and lean less on natural understanding.

Allow your minds to be opened to the supernatural realm to a greater degree than ever before. As your sight gets clearer, ask the Holy Spirit to teach you and help you explore higher places. Above all, remember it is the Holy Spirit who leads us into all truth, He is looking for those who will allow themselves to be led beyond their natural understanding. We need to be like Abraham, who having heard the voice of God to go and sacrifice his son, got up early in the morning, saddled his donkey, and set out to the place of sacrifice. Abraham did not delay, he responded quickly. Any walk with God requires the same outlook. We need to be willing to move from where we are now, saddle our donkey, and go on a journey that may involve sacrifice so we can take hold of fresh revelation and understanding from the throne of God.

The Right Framework

Most of us would like to think that we have a good understanding of the Word of God. But as I look back over the last few years I can see that my understanding of Scripture has changed dramatically. Although it is now normal for me to see people released from unforgiveness, vows, and judgments, a few years ago these experiences were virtually unknown in my life. Many of these revelations and the practical outworking have been practiced by some believers for years. Something that was normal for others was outside my framework in God.

I wish I could say that I just embraced the larger framework, the truth is I struggled with the challenges that I faced. I would speak with some of my friends and disagree with their understanding and experience of God. There were many times I would have to go back to my friends and tell them I now agreed with them. I did not understand the power of God and I found it very easy to reject things that were outside my knowledge and comfortable framework. As time went on, the Holy Spirit opened my eyes and spirit. Our life and experience in God will be framed by our revelation of God and His

Word. How we frame our lives is very important. God laid out the principle of framing life in Hebrews where we are told:

> *By faith we understand that the worlds have been framed by the word of God, so that what is seen hath not been made out of things which appear* (Hebrews 11:3 ASV).

When God created the world he framed it by His word. The same principle applies to our lives. The framework of our lives can easily be the limiting point for us. Church history has many heroes of faith who saw something new in Scripture and embraced it. Often they were strongly persecuted by the establishment for their radical views. In fact, it wasn't long ago that those who spoke in tongues were considered unusual. Now this gift is exercised by believers from wide-ranging backgrounds. After one generation breaks through in an area, though, often the next generation is limited by this framework and unable to embrace fresh revelation. We need to keep the wineskin of our lives flexible.

Eyes That See

Can you imagine being the prophet Elisha? One day Elisha was working in a field when Elijah walked by and threw his cloak around him. Elijah walked on and Elisha had to run after him. Elisha was faced with one of those God encounters—he could stay within a familiar framework or embrace the Word of God and enter a whole new lifestyle. He decided to embrace the road ahead of him with a flourish. He slaughtered the oxen and used his plowing equipment to cook them. He set off to be Elijah's servant. He was later described as the man who poured water on the hands of Elijah. He had a great mentor in Elijah, and was able to watch his ministry closely.

I believe that God wants us to be mentored in every area concerning the things of the Kingdom. Our mentoring should come initially from the Holy Spirit and He will use not one but many people as part of our mentoring process to maturity of faith.

Elisha walked with his mentor to the very end although there must have been times when he felt that he had enough experience to go out on his own. But he knew that his calling in God could only be fulfilled if he stayed with Elijah to the end. Pressure on him increased on that last day when everyone tried to get him to stop following Elijah. Not wavering he received the double portion that he had been looking for and started his ministry where Elijah left off by using the cloak to part the River Jordan.

Although there are no specific references to how it happened, Elisha learned how to see what was happening in the heavenly realms. This was part of his training school with Elijah! His discernment in this area is dramatically revealed in Second Kings chapter 6.

During a war between the Arameans and the Israelites, the king of Aram was very confused and angry because all of his plans were being thwarted. Unknown to the king, God spoke to Elisha about the plans and he warned the king of Israel, enabling him to plan his actions based on the Word of God, and saving his life.

This happened so often that it got to the point when the king of Aram believed that there was a traitor in the camp who was telling his enemies every detail of his plans. But his men knew what was going on. They told the king of Aram that the prophet Elisha knew even the words he spoke in his bedroom. It amuses me that the king of Aram took time to secretly discover where Elisha was living. Surely he would have realized that God would have told Elisha what the king was doing! When the king discovered where Elisha was he sent his army to find and capture him. Although the king was only after one man he sent out his chariots and a strong force to capture him. He clearly thought that if they traveled at night while the prophet was asleep he would not know they were coming and he would be captured in the early morning.

The prophet was so relaxed and peaceful that he did not rush outside first thing in the morning. Instead, it was the prophet's servant who got up early and went out—maybe expecting to have a gentle stroll with God to start the day. As he looked around him, he was immediately faced with a large army surrounding the city. What was he going to do? At this point the servant did not have a heavenly view and had no resource within himself to respond to the situation. He totally panicked and returned to Elisha who was totally unfazed by this latest development.

Elisha confidently made this amazing statement:

> *"Don't be afraid," the prophet answered. "Those who are with us are more than those who are with them." And Elisha prayed, "O Lord, open his eyes so that he may see..."* (2 Kings 6:16-17).

Elisha could not have made this statement without the eyes of his heart being open to everything that was going on in the heavenly realm. It is possible that these might have been the same chariots and horses of fire that appeared when Elijah was taken up to heaven.

It was early morning and he was fully aware of what was happening. His confidence was not locked into earthly things and he had his eyes fixed on Heaven. This Old Testament prophet had been trained by God to see the full picture. His awareness of the picture had a dramatic effect on his response to the predicament in which he found himself.

If he only saw the natural situation he would have reacted like his servant, fearing sudden disaster. In the natural, his position was dangerously serious; in a short time he would be captured. But Elisha could already see the heavenly forces working to bring a great victory. He did not respond in fear, he responded in faith and peace. He trusted God for the outcome. He was probably, like God, laughing at his enemies and their futile attempts to gain the upper hand.

His first statement makes it clear that fear was not an option. The servant had every reason to fear and I am sure that Elisha's statement did not change his thinking at that time. Elisha then said that he had a greater army on his side. Again, this would have been hard to grasp, two men against an entire army does not speak of a great victory. Elisha's prayer is very significant as he asked the Lord to open his servant's eyes. He was not going to miss this opportunity to train the next generation in the heavenly principle of seeing. The servant's eyes were opened:

> *...Then the Lord opened the servant's eyes, and he looked and saw the hills full of horses and chariots of fire all round Elisha* (2 Kings 6:17).

Suddenly the servant had a totally different picture to focus on. His eyes had been opened, but he still had to take the time to look and see. If he had not looked out to the hills he would have missed the army of God that was there. We can pray and ask God to open our eyes but we have to be willing to take the time to look and see. If we don't, then we will miss the very things that God wants to show us.

The servant must have felt totally different after his eyes were opened and he looked around at the fiery armies in the hills. A sense of adventure returned, the fear and danger lifted. It is easier to think positively when you know that you are on the winning side. It is easy to laugh when the victory is assured. The words of Elisha would have made sense. He would have started thinking about what God might be doing in this situation.

How often do we end up in places where even a small glimpse of the heavenly plans would totally change our outlook? The hills are full of the angelic heavenly realms. They are the ministering spirits sent to serve those who inherit salvation. Elisha took charge of the situation as the enemy came toward him, he asked God to take away their natural sight—which he did. He led them to the Israelite king. The final victory was assured and the armies of Aram stopped raiding the Israelites' territory. One man with his eyes open to the heavens was able to end a war and bring the peace to the land.

Even if we are not currently able to see or perceive His angels, let's not forget them. They are working on our behalf, guarding, protecting, and advancing the plans of Heaven around us. We can be like the servant—ask God to open the eyes of our hearts.

A Time to Pray

Before reading on, please join me and engage your faith. Let's ask God to make this your own personal adventure. We can pray together a couple of prayers in the Bible. Don't just visit them once but meditate on them and allow them to become a deep expression of your heart. First, there is the prayer of Elisha, short and simple:

Open my eyes, Lord, that I may see (See 2 Kings 6:17).

The other prayer that I often use for myself and for the local church comes from Ephesians. Because the Spirit caused Paul to write this in the Bible, it must be a prayer that reflects the very heart of God.

I keep asking that the God of our Lord Jesus Christ, the glorious Father, may give you the Spirit of wisdom and revelation, so that you may *know him better. I pray also that the **eyes of your heart may be en-** **lightened** in order that you may know the hope to which he has called you, the riches of his glorious inheritance in the the saints, and his in- comparably great power for us who believe...*(Ephesians 1:17-19 emphasis added).

After you have prayed this prayer, take a few minutes to read some of the supernatural stories in the Bible. For instance, read in the Old Testament about the burning bush (Exod. 3:1-14); the ten plagues (Exod. 8:14–12:30); Elijah fed by ravens (1 Kings 17:1-6); and the dead raised to life (1 Kings 17:17-24; 2 Kings 4:8-37); 2 Kings 13:21). And in the New Testament: walking on the sea (John 6:16-21); tax money in the fish's mouth (Matt. 17:24-27); curing leprosy (Mark 1:40-45); healing an invalid (John 5:1-18). Let your imagina- tion engage the testimonies and provoke your faith.

Chapter 2

LIFE AND DEATH

There are a number of occasions in the Bible when angels are sent by God to rescue people. They make the difference between life and death. The following story is of a time when my life was saved by angelic intervention. This time has had a lasting effect on my life—my confidence in God to keep me safe rocketed!

It was the end of a good day; I had driven in our family car to visit a friend, Michael. During the 100-mile trip the windshield wiper had broken so between provoking and encouraging each other in the things of God we had found a mechanic who had made the necessary repairs.

I was at a time in my spiritual journey when I would regularly find myself pushed beyond my comfort zones. My eyes were constantly being opened to the many unusual and miraculous things that God was doing. It was during these visits with Michael that I began to realize that God could do far more than I could ever ask or imagine. God was not limited by my experience of Him and He was clearly committed to enlarging my outlook—particularly in the realms of the eternal and the supernatural. By His Spirit He made people appear drunk, laugh for hours, and find healing both physically and emotionally.

Unknown to me at this time I was just about to embark on a remarkable lesson in the supernatural—even though I had not been near any church gathering that day—a lesson on the knife edge of life and death.

Encountering Angels

We were very pleased with our family car. My wife and I had only had it for a year and it was a definite improvement over any previous vehicle we owned—in fact, was the answer to prayer. The seven-seat vehicle not only enabled us to transport our family of five but had available space to offer lifts to others.

I said goodbye to Michael and set off for home earlier than normal that evening, aiming to get there in time for my wife and her friend to make a rare visit to the movie theater. The skies turned dark early that day as the cold winter weather had taken hold. The thick, rolling clouds had not given the sun access at any point during the day. The roads were wet with the heavy rain, and every dip in the road was a gathering point for the excess water trapped by overloaded drains. The flooded roads demanded caution as conditions made driving difficult.

The poor weather could not stop the daily rush hour traffic, though, and drivers ignored the pounding rain while racing to their homes. At one point on the route traffic was diverted to avoid the emergency services gathered around an accident that was blocking the road. The weather continued to worsen. The recently fixed windshield wipers could not handle the downpour and the driver's side wiper broke again.

I stopped the car and tried to fix the broken wiper. I am not known for my mechanical abilities; in fact they are non-existent. Earlier in the day I had watched the garage mechanic fix the wiper; he wasn't confident that the repair would last very long. My efforts were less successful than his and it worked only until the next cloud burst. I was getting desperate as I stopped for the third time. The rain was blowing in a horizontal pattern across the road and my waterproof coat was no match for the drenching storm. I stood beside the car soaked to the skin.

I lifted the hood of the car, looking even more like a failed mechanic this time, I pulled out my only tools—a small piece of string and a pocket pen knife. The attempt to repair the problem from the driver's side was totally unsuccessful so I moved around to the passenger's side of the car. With my head buried under the hood I looked hopelessly at the two ends of the broken mechanism and my little piece of string. But at least part of me was dry and I had a bit of thinking time.

As I tried to tie the two parts together I suddenly became aware of the blinding lights of a fast moving car. There was the screech of brakes, then a moment's silence as the lights glided toward me. I watched the slow motion, silent movie through the windshield, like a stunned deer caught by the glare. The first impact hit the back of the car, and then a crunch from a precise blow to the side.

Miraculously I was watching the concluding scene from the other side of the crash barrier at the top of the slope. I watched the offending car twist around in the road and then ram head-on into the remains of our car. The hood closed with a slam and the front parts of the car, including the bumper, were ripped off by the impact.

I watched the other vehicle as it continued, then ground to a halt about a hundred yards up the road, leaving behind a trail of devastation and debris. It was all over in seconds. Parts of the car were everywhere. I shouted thanks of victory as I left my safe vantage point. Other cars narrowly missed the mangle of metal as they raced around the corner. I made a quick check on the other driver and found him shaken and wandering around aimlessly.

In the flurry of activity that followed it dawned on me that I was not only alive but was somehow uninjured. The gravity of the situation was enhanced by the large number of emergency service vehicles that arrived expecting to find dead and injured. I gave the necessary witness statements and sat in the local police station for an hour waiting for my wife. I was amazed that somehow I had escaped. Although my car appeared unmoved initially, I realized later that it had been jolted off the side of the road and returned back to its original position.

Over the next couple of days the slight pain in my right arm revealed a series of bruises. They looked exactly like the finger prints from a firm grip. I realized that my athletic high jump abilities—lifting myself out from under the hood of the car, jumping upward and backward over the crash barrier, and landing on my feet, had heavenly assistance. My wife said it had to be a miracle because I could not naturally move that fast out of harm's way.

I believe an angel grabbed me by the elbow, lifted me out from under the hood of the car, flung me up the slope, and over the crash barrier—all in a fraction of a second. I knew that God has the ability to do anything; now He had done something outside my personal box. I knew that my life had been preserved by angelic intervention. This encounter with an angel changed my life forever.

So Why Angels?

Questions I am often asked include: what difference do angels make in our daily life and did I notice any changes after my life-saving angel encounter? This story would be incomplete without mentioning some of the consequences of this heavenly intervention. Over the next few weeks I realized that every day of my life had been numbered by God. This was no longer a theory or flippant statement; I knew I was alive due to God's intervention. The Holy Spirit then spoke to me clearly through the Scripture about the importance of the commandment to honor your father and mother. This is a commandment with a promise, that all may go well with you and you will live a long life.

> *"Honor your father and mother"—which is the first commandment with a promise—"that it may go well with you and that you may enjoy long life on the earth"* (Ephesians 6:2-3).

In my mind this command of honoring always seemed disconnected from the attached promise. It felt like some random heavenly edict tagged on the end. Later it became clear that this was not a randomly collated Scripture but part of God's creative laws. In simple terms, to honor our father and mother means to give value to them.

In Genesis Adam and Eve were called to honor their heavenly Father and do the things He had asked them to do. When they took of the fruit of the tree of knowledge of good and evil to gain wisdom they were actively dishonoring their heavenly Father.

The consequences of their action are clear. They immediately lost their right to eternal life and were thrown out of the garden. Then God spoke the curse over them. Things were no longer guaranteed to go well for them. Among the curses that God spoke to Adam are thorns and thistles, sweating to work the ground, and painful toil. It was not long before they experienced the loss of a son through murder. The combination of the power of this Scripture and the fact that God saved my life made me realize that God has a long life available for me.

This revelation was reinforced when a young lady in the local church asked a few weeks later if she could pray that God would give me a long life. Since that confirmation a major change happened in me and I do not question God's ability to keep me safe. I am now happy to go anywhere that God wants me to go. Even if there is danger, I know that I am here until God calls me home, and when He does I am going to a better place anyway. I love the passage in John 14 where Jesus tells us that He is going ahead of us to prepare a place for us. I believe that the Scripture about honoring our parents is a key one in the life of many believers. There are no get-out clauses. If we are going to allow the fullness of the blessing of God to flow in our lives let's make sure we have this area straight!

Accident Fallout

Another result of my supernatural angel encounter became clear over the next few months. After the accident my wife Sue came to collect me from the police station. On the way she told me she pondered the fact that, "I had broken her new car" and a specific prayer emerged from her heart. She prayed not only that we would get a new car but that the patio doors that had been one of her dream improvements to our house would also be provided as a direct result of the accident. These doors would replace a small back window and represented to us that God is the One who would create a way where there is no way. If you knew my wife then you would understand this is the type of thing she will pray, leaving me totally bewildered about how she connected the two things. As I often do in these situations, I smiled at the time not believing that it would happen!

This prayer seemed even more unlikely to be fulfilled due to a dispute that followed with the insurance company over the value of our car. Even though our car was totally unrepairable because of the accident, it appeared that we would have to pay a large sum of money and struggle to purchase a car of similar quality. The dispute rumbled on, and over six weeks later the insurance payout was still not finalized. I was unsuccessful even to persuade the insurance company to make what I thought was a reasonable payout.

While visiting our family over the Easter break we noticed an identical white vehicle for sale beside the road. I had an instant feeling that this was our new car, combined with doubt that this was too good to be true. Up until this time I had always struggled when buying new cars. I had listened to too many stories about people buying cars that turned out to be unreliable. This time I was unsure that God could provide a car so easily!

As usual I found myself challenged by my wife's enthusiasm and determination to buy the car we had just seen. I coolly agreed to take a closer look at the car and lost a good part of a night's sleep trying to think things through! I know that doesn't work—but I did it anyway. The next day we looked over the car and found that it was a significant improvement over our previous car. There was nothing really wrong with it and the last letters on the number plate grabbed our attention: "WHY."

Then we came to the all important question of price. Much to our surprise the man was asking much less than we were trying to get from the insurance company. We knew the price was a very good deal, as it was already less than the expected book value. We both felt that God did not want us to negotiate on price and after a short discussion we were about to offer the full price. Before we could finish, the owner surprised us. He said that he did not want to negotiate either and would reduce the asking price by 10 percent. We had the new car—God continued to organize every detail.

When we contacted the insurance company the person we had been dealing was away for Easter break. His replacement felt that the case had been dragging on far too long and instantly agreed to a payout that was significantly beyond the value of the car that we were buying. The extra money was enough for my wife to start looking for her patio doors. In reality, though, there was still not enough money even to buy the doors, let alone get them fitted. We kept looking and one day we felt the Holy Spirit telling us to go ahead with the doors. While they were in the process of being fitted the insurance company sent a letter offering a significant sum of money to cover the incidental expenses of the accident and the bruising! The total of all the spare money was enough to purchase and fit the patio doors.

In our hearts we felt that God demonstrated how He could prepare a way where there was no way. Nothing is impossible for Him. A couple of days after the doors were installed we completed the lasts bits of redecorating. The following weekend we had a prophet visiting the church for the first time; on Friday evening she started to pray that God would create a way where there was no way. We knew that we had entered a new stage in our journey with God.

Journey Forward

The impact of that time continues to be a significant. It prompted many new questions. This was not the first time that God had intervened. There had been a previous occasion where we were left wondering whether He had sent an angelic visitation to help us out. I had to conclude that God does not intend us to have brief moments when we become aware of the unseen realm but these experiences should be part of our daily lives. In looking at the subject of angels and the heavenly realms there are those who will immediately feel uncomfortable and concerned, they will want to look for the balance. While agreeing that it is important that we find a clear biblical basis, we must not let our caution stop our journey with God.

If Peter had stopped he would never have gone to Cornelius' house, which was against the law. He followed, instead, the leading of the Holy Spirit, enjoyed visions, visitors directed by angels, and then a fresh Pentecost experience in the house of Cornelius. (See Acts 10.) The full revelation came after the experience. If we want to break out of our boxes and journey forward into the fullness of God's supernatural realms we must learn to trust the Holy Spirit with a humble heart. As we do this we admit our mistakes and thank God for the victories as we are led into the full truth.

As with any journey there is the danger of getting a little lost or travelling farther than we needed to on certain roads, but if we never leave home we will never have any real adventures and our opportunities to learn will be limited. I would rather go on the adventure and make honest mistakes than remain stagnant and achieve nothing through caution and fear. One thing you will not find in this book is shortcuts for growth in God. We all like the shortcuts so we get to our destination quicker. Often the church culture today can encourage these shortcuts as we get caught by the results of other people's secret lives with God.

Daily we need to be finding our own secret place of peace with our Heavenly Father and following the journey He is unravelling for us. We can be like Abraham; he knew his final destination as he had seen a heavenly city but he still had to set out on the journey. When Abraham was told to take Isaac up the mountain to be sacrificed, he got up early in the morning and set out! We have our final destination to be with our Heavenly Father forever, let us remember this is a journey and we are allowed to enjoy the process. This book provides signposts so that we do not get lost along the way. It also helps us engage in our heavenly purpose at a higher level. But the book will not make the journey for us!

At the end of this chapter please join me and pray the prayer that Paul wrote in Ephesians. This is a prayer that I often use to focus my attention on the purposes of God. My prayer is that God will do immeasurably more that you ask or imagine and you allow the power of God to work in you and change you on the journey.

I kneel before the Father, from whom His whole family in heaven and on earth derives its name. I pray that out of His glorious riches He may strengthen you with power through His Spirit in your inner being, so that Christ may dwell in your hearts through faith. And I pray that you, being rooted and established in love, may have power, together with all the saints, to grasp how wide and long and high and deep is the love of Christ, and to know this love that surpasses knowledge—that you may be filled to the measure of all the fullness of God. Now to Him *who is **able to do immeasurably more than all we ask or imagine**, according to His power that is at work within us, to Him be glory in the church and in Christ Jesus throughout all generations, for ever and ever! Amen* (Ephesians 3:14-21 emphasis added).

Chapter 3

THE ROAD TO FREEDOM

In the previous chapter I shared a little of my personal story and how God has brought angelic intervention into my life. Now we are going to look at the involvement of the angelic in bringing and maintaining freedom for the believer. While there are many books written on the effects of demonic oppression and possession on people's lives and the benefits of deliverance, there is little about the role of the angelic in the believers' day-to-day freedom and health. When we are born again we enter the gateway into the Kingdom of God, this is the Kingdom of our Heavenly Father. In fact Jesus tells us that, *"no one can see the Kingdom of God unless he is born again"* (John 3:3). Our spirit comes alive and God sends the Holy Spirit to dwell in us and lead us into all truth, He also sends the angels to work with us and bring the Kingdom to us. In Hebrews we learn that the angels are sent to minister to those who have entered the Kingdom.

> *Are not all angels ministering spirits sent to serve those who will inherit salvation?* (Hebrews 1:14)

We are going to look at sonship, the power of forgiveness, the effect of vows, and unresolved anger. We will get glimpses of the role of the heavenly realms in these areas of our lives.

One of the distinctions of the New Testament is the revelation that God is the Heavenly Father: His son is Jesus and when we become believers we are His brothers. When Jesus came to earth He knew that He had been sent by His Father, confirmed when He was baptized and filled with the Holy Spirit. The Spirit led Him into the wilderness for a time of prayer and fasting. When the devil came and tempted Jesus, he understood the power of sonship. Satan said, *"If you are the Son of God..."* (Luke 4:3). Jesus knew He was the Son and did not fall to the temptation.

Paul writes about the sonship of believers on numerous occasions. In his letter to the Ephesians he said that God, *"...In love predestined us to be adopted as his sons through Jesus Christ..."* (Eph. 1:4-5). It is important we realize that in the Kingdom of God there is no distinction made between male and female, and He calls all believers His sons. This is shown clearly in Galatians 3:26-28:

> *You are all sons of God through faith in Christ Jesus, for all of you who were baptized into Christ have clothed yourselves with Christ. There is neither Jew nor Greek, slave nor free, male nor female, for you are all one in Christ Jesus.*

This is a vital revelation in the life of the believer. I have seen when the revelation of sonship comes to believers—their lives are transformed and fresh confidence emerges. When our confidence in our sonship grows, so does our understanding of our authority on earth. This is clearly written in Romans:

> *For you did not receive a spirit that makes you a slave again to fear, but you received the Spirit of sonship. And by him we cry, "Abba, Father." The Spirit Himself testifies with our spirit that we are God's children. Now if we are children, then we are heirs—heirs of God and co-heirs with Christ, if indeed we share in His sufferings in order that we may also share in His glory* (Romans 8:15-17).

In society today this is one of the critical issues constantly undermined by satan, making it harder for believers to embrace their identities as sons. If you are not clear about your place as a son of God then ask the Holy Spirit to bring this revelation clearly to you. This is a foundational revelation that the Holy Spirit is committed to reveal to you. I believe that the Holy Spirit is constantly reminding us of our sonship. I know that as a dad I am constantly reminding my children that God has given them to me and how much I love them. We are told that having a child-like attitude is vital for us to understand the things of the Kingdom.

Servants and Family

One evening while I was away from home God brought the importance of sonship and its relationship to the angelic home to me. I was just drifting off to sleep thinking about the way God had been setting people free and demonstrating His love in extravagant ways. Suddenly God played a movie scene in my mind. (God sometimes speaks to me in this way, usually the images stay with me and I start to understand them as I meditate on them.)

As I replayed the scene over the next few days, God brought more and more revelation. I had found myself joining the scene taking place in a traditional old English house. It was the type of place owned by the wealthy gentry of previous generations. Incidentally, there is one of these homes very close to where I live; it is open to the public and I have walked through on a number of occasions.

The backdrop of the scene God gave me is lavish, designed to impress rich guests. The rooms are grand with the walls adorned with large pictures of previous owners, and unique artifacts showcasing the owner's wealth. The house is surrounded by immaculate gardens, everything in straight lines that could be seen from all the main rooms of the house. There is a long, winding drive lined with trees, leading to the house; giving the visitor every opportunity to see the owner's splendid estate.

In the first scene of my picture I am in the basement kitchens of the house. Because the owner and his guests would never have ventured into this area there are no beautiful decorations or luxury that exist upstairs. The kitchen area is clean, with all the cooking utensils hung neatly on the walls, but the whole scene is grey. I am one of the most junior servants in the house and I find myself standing before the head servant. He has been given authority to make sure everything runs correctly according to the master's orders. I instinctively knew that when he gave any orders I had to obey very quickly. I was certainly not allowed to go upstairs to the main house without his permission; even then I was not expected to be seen by the master of the house.

The head servant ordered me to follow him up the stairs with a tray of things. The stairs were almost hidden in the corner of the room and reflected the rest of the downstairs area, clean but grey and dreary. I was nervous following the boss up the narrow, twisting stairs. When we reached the top, the door opened out into a room filled with amazing colors; the reds were rich and luxurious, golds and deep wood panelling lined the walls. Although I had been given authority to be in this part of the house I knew I did not belong. I was only a servant and had no authority here.

Suddenly the picture changed and so did my place in the house. I was no longer the servant; I am the son of the house. I now have the authority and the right to be in the upstairs of the house. I made my own decisions, immediately realizing that the position of a son is dramatically different. I felt different, I acted differently, I even looked different. I felt colorful, not grey. Life completely changed just because I had a different position on the inside of myself. I felt like I was the head and not the tail. I was still not the owner of the house; the house belonged to my loving Father. The parallels between this scene and my relationship with God were quite startling. There is a big difference between a servant and a son. As Jesus said:

> *"I no longer call you servants, because a servant does not know his master's business. Instead I have called you my friends, for everything that I learned from my Father I have made known to you"* (John 15:15).

In the vision I took my place as a son to heart and suddenly the servants appeared. They had been given the authority and a responsibility to serve me, the son of the house owner. They were to look out for me and make life easier in every way. I sat down in a large chair and started to enjoy the lavish setting and the privileges. As I looked more closely I realized that the servants were in fact angels. I was reminded that the angels had been given the authority to serve those who inherit salvation. I watched the angels come into the room and saw they were all carrying things from Heaven. They were there to bring healing and restoration from the Heavenly Father to me, to the believers. Some of them were even carrying different parts of the body which spoke to me of their involvement in creative miracles.

Even as I consider this vision again I am reminded of my privilege of being a son of God and the authority that is released to me as His son. We all, as sons, have the full support of the angelic realms in helping us walk free in every aspect of our lives—as this vision powerfully illustrated to me. When I do not embrace my place, I live like the servant under the stairs.

Forgiveness and the Angels

Over the past few years I have realized that I am able to affect the spiritual activity around my life by my attitudes and by having a heart full of grace and forgiveness. I have recently joined my friend Duncan Smith on a couple of visits to Kyrgyzstan. The Christian church in that nation is relatively new and the faith of the people is raw and radical. We found they were desperate for fresh encounters with God and did not have the baggage that can so often stop us from allowing the power of God to flow in our lives and meetings.

During our two visits we ministered the message of the Father's love and the importance of forgiveness. The power of God broke out over the people as they readily responded. There were many tears as they repented and forgave those who had treated them harshly. Many came free from the strongholds of ancestral worship. As they responded passionately we saw great liberty come, hundreds of demons flee, and many instant dramatic healings. The evidence of angelic activity was all over the room as satan's power was broken. It was during these meetings that God sent signs to show His presence. In one meeting we saw feathers fall from heaven, gold dust appeared on people's hands, faces, and on the ground around them. These were signs manifested from Heaven, as God was bringing freedom to His people. The fruit of this time was evident through the many testimonies of healing and freedom—the deaf heard, the blind saw, and those tormented with demons were freed.

I considered why the simple act of forgiveness should have such a dramatic effect, far beyond what we might expect. Healing came as a result of forgiveness, lives dramatically changed. There appeared to be far more going on than an internal transaction of the heart.

I looked in some detail at the parable Jesus told about the king who wanted to settle up his accounts with the servants (Matt. 18:23-35). In this parable both demonic and angelic activity are released through forgiveness from the heart. The king started calling his servants in and a man came in who owed him ten thousand talents, which is a bit like owing a few million dollars—a debt impossible to repay. As the king demanded that his rules be enacted and the servant and his whole family were sold into slavery, the servant cried out for mercy. He begged for the opportunity to pay everything back; a promise impossible to keep. The king decided to cancel the entire debt and let the man go. This example is a great picture of salvation and how Jesus clears all our sin and lets us go. When we turn to God, the change in our lives not only affects us but our whole family.

The man left the presence of the king and went looking for a fellow servant who owed him a small amount of money. He grabbed this man and started to throttle him. It is clear that the generosity of the king had not changed his heart. He did not heed the cries of his fellow servant who asked for the same mercy that the king had just shown. He refused to listen and had the man thrown into prison until he was able to pay off everything that he owed. There was not even the smallest hint of compassion.

We can be indignant at the behavior of the man, yet at the same time we can get caught in the same trap. It is important that we take a few moments to examine our own hearts for areas of unforgiveness, or when we have treated someone harshly. These issues, left unresolved, will cause major blocks of the blessings of God. We can release far greater angelic activity in our lives by forgiving and putting any outstanding issues right.

The sin of the servant was soon brought to the attention of the king by the other servants who were upset at what was happening. The king called the servant back in and made it clear that his act of grace and generosity should have been enough for the servant to apply the same principle to the person who owed him money. The master then had the servant given over to be tortured, *until he paid back all he owed.*

Jesus makes this statement *"This is how my heavenly Father will treat each of you unless you forgive your brother from your heart"* (Matt. 18:35).

This is not just a story but a principle of the kingdom. The king in his kindness does not reinstate his original debt. Our heavenly Father is like that with us, He does not reinstate our sin, He chooses to forget. The King is looking at today's issues. As it says in the Lord's Prayer: *"Forgive us our debts, as we also have forgiven our debtors"* (Matt. 6:12).

Our acts of forgiveness release forgiveness from Heaven. The servant in this parable had a debt outstanding. All he had to do was to release his fellow servant from prison and forgive the full debt. It was something that he could do very easily with a change of heart. At this point the principle of sowing and reaping comes into play—he took another's freedom and he lost his own.

There was another consequence of his actions. He was going to be tortured, which speaks to the open door for demonic attack. When we do not forgive, we open ourselves up to a wide array of problems that have their origin in the spiritual realm. If you do not want trespassers coming into your house then you must close the door, otherwise it is an invitation to enter. If we are aware of areas of unforgiveness in our lives then we have opened the door for satan and his minions to have a field day. It is important to take time to deal fully with this unforgiveness. The Bible shows clearly how the spiritual realm interacts with our daily lives when we do not forgive.

How much more angelic activity is released through forgiveness? Demons are only fallen angels. As we remove their right to affect our lives in any way, we open our lives to the impact of angelic help. As we do everything with a pure heart we release ourselves to operate in the Kingdom economy that includes the angelic.

Vows and the Angelic

The principles of how the spiritual realms interact with our lives is again clearly illustrated by the opportunity that satan is afforded by our words. We need to understand that satan will try and draw us into things that he can then use to tie up our lives. He will always use the principles of Heaven—and pervert them.

Jesus says:

> *Do not swear at all: either by heaven, for it is God's throne; or by the earth, for it is his footstool; or by Jerusalem, for it is the city of the Great King. And do not swear by your head, for you cannot make even one hair white or black. Simply let your "Yes" be "Yes," and your "No," "No"; anything beyond this comes from the evil one* (Matthew 5:34-37).

This passage of scripture might seem rather harsh at first glance. It is clear that as soon as we go beyond the simple statement of yes or no and make a vow, we are opening a door that allows satan to tie us up. Satan simply tries to draw us into saying things that he can use to steal our freedom. This is the same thing he has been doing since the Fall in the Garden of Eden.

I have seen many people whose statements have been used by satan to tie them up. In this book I do not intend to go into great depth about how to be free; but, I will give a few illustrations and testimonies so we can understand how this principle works. When we understand, then we are in a place to close the door on satan's activities and open the door to angelic activity in and around our lives.

Often vows are made for what appear to be very good reasons, maybe we have been hurt badly and feel the need to protect ourselves from ever being hurt again. As soon as we make a vow we are actually saying that we do not need God's protection in our lives as we will be strong enough to look after ourselves; thereby opening a door for satan to tie us up again and again.

I have spoken to people on numerous occasions who have told me about bullying at work. Delving deeper we discover that this is a pattern that has gone on for most of their lives. Often there was a point when the person vowed never to let anyone hurt them again. By making this statement of independence they opened a door that satan uses to cause bullies to come at them from all directions throughout their lifetime. To break this cycle we first have to understand that God will protect and look after us. The Psalmist states this well:

Hear my cry, O God; listen to my prayer. From the ends of the earth I call to you, I call as my heart grows faint; lead me to the rock that is higher than I. For you have been my refuge, a strong tower against the foe. I long to dwell in your tent forever and take refuge in the shelter of your wings. Selah (Psalm 61:1-4).

Elsewhere he writes:

He who dwells in the shelter of the Most High will rest in the shadow of the Almighty. I will say of the Lord, "He is my refuge and my fortress, my God, in whom I trust." Surely he will save you from the fowler's snare and from the deadly pestilence. He will cover you with his feathers, and under his wings you will find refuge; his faithfulness will be your shield and rampart (Psalm 91:1-4).

When we understand that God is our protection, we are able to set ourselves free from our statements of independence. By doing this we close the door on the enemy and open ourselves to the blessing of God. We have seen when people are freed from bullies by forgiving and breaking vows made years before. There have even been times when people are aware of being delivered as they dealt with the issues in their heart. Now I always pray for the blessing of God and ask that the angels will come and minister complete healing and blessing.

I remember seeing one person break some of the statements made against a parent. Over the next week or two the blessings of God that emerged were far beyond just saying a few words—she regained health and made positive life-changing decisions. Her life was opened to the angels of God, who worked the blessing of God through him.

This principle is also reflected in Matthew 18:18 when Jesus tells us that, *"Whatever you bind on earth will be bound in heaven, and whatever you loose on earth will be loosed in heaven."* God has given us the authority of sons; we need to make sure that we are using this authority in line with Heaven's economy.

A number of times I have spoken to people who are struggling to sell their homes. They have houses that would normally sell easily but for various reasons the house doesn't sell. In some cases we have found that the person has made a statement of ownership that has allowed the enemy to hold them to the house even though it is God's plan for them to move on. These statements have included, "I will always live here," and "My children will always have a home here." As soon as these statements were broken on earth it released the will of God and the enemy could no longer put a stop on the plans of God.

These type of vows are stated in many different ways but if they take us away from depending on God then we are cooperating unnecessarily with the enemy. The words may seem reasonable or true but they actually form a foothold that will lock us up with the enemy and away from God's plan.

Anger and Angels

"In your anger do not sin": Do not let the sun go down while you are still angry, and do not give the devil a foothold (Ephesians 4:26-27).

The devil needs a foothold to influence our lives, angels don't! I do not live life thinking that the devil is having a go at me. I know that unless I give him a foothold then he can not touch me. When you look at the life of Jesus you realize that satan could not touch him. Jesus came through the temptations untouched and He lived His life on earth untouched. Even when He was betrayed this was determined by God, Jesus gave Himself up and allowed Himself to go to the cross—at the cross He gave up His spirit. There were no gaps, no sin that gave the devil a foothold.

The scripture in Ephesians tells us not to give the devil somewhere in our lives where he can place his evil foot. Although I am not a rock climber and have no desire to navigate my way up a rock face, a number of years ago I had an opportunity to learn the importance of footholds. I was part of an outreach team that spent a couple of days in a local mountain range. The smallest mountain would have been beyond my ability on a nice summer's day but our enthusiastic leader was actually taking us out on a very cold, snowy February morning. I had borrowed as much clothing as possible, wearing a bright orange overall with a smooth shiny surface. The first part of the day was an easy walk along well-established paths. We were following our athletic leader who had us climbing up one of the snowy slopes—which confirmed to me that heights and climbing were not my thing. I did not have the ability to make the necessary footholds to stay on the mountain and it was not long before I found myself hanging on the snowy slope by my fingers. I lost my grip and with the help of my slick, shiny jacket went body boarding back down the hill. I did not have the necessary footholds to stay on the hill!

If satan does not have a foothold in our lives he will slide off as well. If we hold onto unresolved anger then we provide a foothold in our lives that satan can take advantage of. It is very simple to close the door and remove the opportunity. We need to turn away from our anger through repentance. There are many different areas of sin that can provide footholds; we need to ask the Holy Spirit to reveal them to us so we can deal with them.

As I said earlier, angels do not need footholds, they are sent to serve the sons of God. As we serve God they are assigned to help and strengthen us as we fulfill our purpose in God. I believe that the issues covered in this chapter are vital areas for us to consider in living our lives in God. I have not covered the principles in great detail but give a taste of the freedom that is available for each believer. The work of Jesus is to heal everyone oppressed of the devil. If we do not take time to resolve these fundamental things in our lives then we limit His blessings, the activity of the angelic, and the supernatural. We also cause stumbling blocks that affect the lives of people around us.

Our character is of fundamental importance to God as the Scripture tells us to be imitators of Him in every way. We can have the sharpest seeing gift but it will not profit the Body of Christ if we allow the issues of unforgiveness to go unresolved. Our vision will be tainted and not pure as God intends. My desire is that the Body of Christ sees clearly and partners with the heavenly realms from pure hearts. Take time to pray and ask the Holy Spirit to work through any issues in your heart.

Chapter 4

GOING OFF THE MAP

Many of us may not realize that the angels have names that represent their responsibilities and roles—similar to Old Testament characters who were named and renamed according to their destiny.

As a family we were at the end of a busy time; our youngest daughter, Abbie, had been in the hospital with suspected appendicitis. My wife and I were relieved that it turned out not to be serious. Although our daughter had some longer term medical issues, I had always been confident that God was looking after her and would see · her through. After this stay in the hospital I found that for the first time a fear of her suffering a more serious illness had crept into my mind and affected my heart.

Shortly thereafter I attended a conference ready to be refreshed outside the things of daily life. During the first day I was challenged by the Holy Spirit to deal with some issues that I was holding in my heart. When the speaker finished and invited people to come forward for prayer I made my way to the front ready to resolve these things. I knew that the presence of God was strong in the meeting

49

but at this point I was more aware of myself and my own heart. Having processed these issues and come to a place of repentance and resolve, the person ministering continued to pray.

Suddenly the person declared that God was going to give me a finance angel to bring supernatural resources to the ministry. I must admit that I was delighted with this word and immediately thought of loads of different assignments that I could ask God to send this angel on. This angel would be busy! As the person prayed I became aware of not just the angel of finance standing in front of me but I was even more conscious of two other angels standing on either side. I could not see them with my natural eyes but I could see where they were standing and recognize their outline with my heart's eyes. I was now aware of the closeness of God and as I stood in His presence I started to ask the Holy Spirit to bring revelation.

My Daughter's Angel

The Holy Spirit started to speak into my heart. I felt him say that my daughter's angel, on the left, was called Abigail. He also told me that I had been shown this angel so that I would know that God was looking after her. I found it strange that this angel would be called Abigail as I only ever thought of my little girl as Abbie. We had been so particular about her name we made sure that Abbie was on her birth certificate. I would not even have turned my head if someone had called her Abigail. The presence of this angel suddenly made sense of why so many people called her Abigail even after I introduce her by her birth name—Abbie. At this point something in my heart changed, I no longer felt concerned about Abbie's health. I regained my confidence that God was looking after her and was thankful that she had an angel assigned to her.

I have been aware of the presence of this angel on one other occasion since then. The rest of my family had been away visiting grandparents. On the day they were returning home I realized the angel Abigail was traveling around in the car with me. God was demonstrating again that he was in charge. It did not surprise me later to find that Abbie had been sick while away but was fully recovered.

The Holy Spirit also spoke to me about the second angel who was standing on the right when he first appeared. He told me his name was Alexander and I would find out about him from Alexander the Great. I was a bit stumped at this point, my knowledge of history is very limited and I was still struggling with angels having names. I put this to the back of my mind knowing that, in His perfect time, God would have to authenticate the experience I had just had.

Angel of Finance

I was really excited at the thought of having an angel of finance around and decided to ask God to send him on a mission. I wanted to prove that he existed and that I was not suffering from a distorted imagination. I did not tell anyone except my wife about the angel or my prayers. My most pressing need was to get the money to cover the airfares for a team of people who had recently traveled with me. My first prayer was that God would send his angel to provide these airfares. It was not a lot of money and I knew there were a few people around who God could prompt to give it!

A couple of days later the money arrived, but not from any local source. There was another check with my name on it included in the envelope. As I read the note attached I found this extra money was not to line my own pockets but was a gift for one of the team members to help them with their airfare for a future visit to Africa. I was very encouraged with this start so I then asked God to release the finance angel to the bigger task of clearing the mortgage of our local church building. I thought that this was going to be a very interesting challenge as it went beyond the spare money someone would have and I was not planning to make an appeal. I was staggered when someone came into my office a few days later and asked me the value of the outstanding mortgage on the building as they felt that God was prompting them to pay off the mortgage. This transaction was completed within a short period. Over the next year there were numerous stories of God's provision that came to fulfill specific financial needs both small and large. I was quickly convinced that the angel was real and active.

Time to Go Off the Map

The other angel, called Alexander, was a bit of a mystery to me. A little while later I was reading a book that I had purchased at the same angelic-encounter conference. The book, *When Heaven Invades Earth* by Bill Johnson, had already become the most significant one I had read that year. Suddenly I was struck by the words, "History provides us with a lesson...." As I read on, the author spoke about Alexander the Great and how he had won victory after victory until he reached the foot of the Himalayas. Here he went to the captains of his armies and challenged them to go over the mountains into the uncharted territory. The captains were uncertain about this farther adventure but eventually agreed to follow Alexander off the map.[1]

The Holy Spirit immediately spoke into my heart about the angel Alexander. His role is to take us all into the greater adventures and victories which are found in uncharted territory. We can think that we have experienced everything that God want us to and if something is outside our experience we get cautious, even critical. Even if we have already experienced great victories God wants to take us further in the journey. God wants us to go off the map to uncharted places. We need to allow the Holy Spirit to lead us forward with the help of His angels. There are so many adventures and exciting things that God wants us to do.

We can read people's stories and wish they would happen to us. The good news is that there are loads of new adventures that have never been written about. There are victories that God has just for you if you are willing to go off the map. I have always enjoyed new adventures with God. I came to realize that when the angel Alexander appeared in a meeting, or at any other time, God was preparing to lead us off our map of experience. All I had to do was to follow his leading. On occasions I am aware of the angel coming into meetings to minister to people and I know we are going to enter a fresh place in God at that time.

In one meeting just before I was scheduled to speak I realized that the angel Alexander had walked in the back of the room. I stood up but had not spoken a word. The angel walked across the back of the room and many people, unaware of what was going on in the spirit realm, were filled with the joy and laughter of God. Many people were released, including someone who had for years been unable to find freedom from a demon. That day I understood more than ever, it is not by natural wisdom that we learn. We do not have to understand everything. God simply wants us to give Him room to do things His way. Let the ministering spirits—the angels—minister. I decided at that point to ask God to keep taking me off the map as that is where some of the greatest adventures and discoveries are in Him. Since then the level of the supernatural increased and there have been many supernatural events, healings, and unusual prophetic events.

Learning to Be Led

One wet day during our Christmas holidays I was given a visual demonstration of the way the angel Alexander can lead us. I went out early to walk our puppy with my daughter, Abbie, who was then 5 years old. She was already known for her strong opinions and she was not someone who would normally enjoy walking up a steep hill, even with the dog. We followed the narrow road up through the woods. I started thinking back about the many times while I was in high school when I ran cross country up the steep incline.

Suddenly my daughter declared that she did not want to walk up the path but wanted to take an alternative route directly up the hill. Initially I refused to join her adventure; the main path was steep enough without fighting up steep muddy slopes around the protruding tree roots. Eventually she persuaded me that I needed to follow her lead. We needed each other to even stand up in the winter mud. We grabbed hold of trees and invented our route up the hill. At times we had to fight through the brambles. It felt as if we were somewhere that no one had ever been before; we were adventurers making many discoveries on the way.

Over an hour later we found a way out at the top of the hill into the open space, laughing at the fun that we had had together. Immediately after we came into the open Abbie wanted to return back down the hill. The well-worn paths held no attraction for her. We set off back through the shrub and into the wood. We slid and laughed our way back down the hill; we were muddy and cold but excited to get home and tell everyone about our explorations.

Soon we were back on the path and I knew that I would have missed a very special time with my daughter if I had stayed on the safe and sensible route. As I walked the last few yards to the house the Holy Spirit spoke in my heart. Did I enjoy going off the map? Did I mind getting a little dirty? Did I feel closer to my daughter? I began to understand a little more about the journey that God has for us. His angelic assignment for each one of us is to take us off the map and enable us to have our own unique journey through life, experiencing supernatural encounters.

Will you go off the map with God? This is the mark of the early New Testament church when angels are normal, buildings shake, there are visions and dreams, and even divine transportation. There is a feeling that God can do anything.

Follow the Adventurers of Faith

A quick review of the many Godly people in the Bible will help us realize that the ability to live off the map was a characteristic of all the men and women of faith. The cloud of witnesses listed in Hebrews 11 shows how many had allowed their eyes to be caught up with the eternal realms. We are told that Abraham was willing to be a wanderer as he had seen a heavenly city whose architect and builder was God himself. There are many characters who only get a brief mention but are also part of those willing to live off the early map.

One of my favorite characters is Benaiah (2 Sam. 23:20). He was listed as one of David's mighty men. I love his zeal which meant that on a snowy day he had to go off the normal map and create his own adventure. On a day when most of us would throw a few snowballs and run back inside to enjoy a hot drink in front of a warm fire, Benaiah went down a pit and killed a lion. This dramatic act demonstrated an extraordinary faith. When we step off the map and live in the realms of faith we have not only the assistance and back-up of the

Holy Spirit working within us but the angelic realms are activated to serve us as well.

Endnote

1. Johnson, Bill. *When Heaven Invades Earth,* (Shippensburg, PA: Treasure House, 2003), 75-76.

Chapter 5

IN THE BEGINNING

Have you ever stopped to think about the world before the Fall? Have you ever considered what things looked like through the eyes of Adam and Eve? Before you read on, why not take a bit of time to look at the first three chapters of Genesis. Look at the story of Adam and Eve from their eyes until the time they are thrown out of the garden.

Chances are you noticed that the world looked radically different from the way we see things today. Our eyes have become dim to many aspects of God's creation and there are many things that have changed as a result of sin. This change is clearly stated in Romans 8, which says creation has been subjected to frustrations since the Fall. The effect of sin brought the world into bondage. The plan of God liberates the world.

The creation waits in eager expectation for the sons of God to be re-vealed. For the creation was subjected to frustration, not by its own choice, but by the will of the one who subjected it, in hope that the cre-ation itself will be liberated from its bondage to decay and brought into

57

*the glorious freedom of the children of God. We know that the whole
creation has been groaning as in the pains of childbirth right up to the
present time* (Romans 8:19-22).

The Book of Genesis gives us many insights into the world before
the Fall. It is the seed book of the Bible, containing many of the principles that are foundational to the Kingdom of God. As we move
through the Scriptures these seed revelations are developed and
brought into fullness through Christ. I would like to spend a few moments looking at the world and at what was visible to Adam and Eve
at creation.

This is one of those times when we need to think outside our normal patterns to be able to embrace the world from their viewpoint.
Our ways of thinking have been trained in the patterns of the world
and need to be renewed in the patterns of the Kingdom of God. As
we read the creation account we see that God was creating the heavens and the earth at the same time. At this point there was no divid-
ing line caused by sin. God had already planned in His heart to
make Adam and Eve in the image of the full Godhead.

He took some of the dust of the earth He had created and started
to mold Adam in His hands as a potter would take a piece of clay
and mold it into the shape He had seen in his heart. He was the potter working with great precision as in every detail Adam would re-
flect the image of the Godhead. This was the greatest work of art
that had ever taken place. The Lord then breathed life into his nos-
trils (Gen. 2:7). This made mankind different from all of creation.
The animals were only made from the earth and the angels were
spiritual beings. Adam and Eve were made from the earth and yet
were made spiritually alive with the breath of God.

Then God spoke a powerful prophetic blessing over His new creation: *"Be fruitful and increase in number; fill the earth and subdue it. Rule
over the fish of the sea and the birds of the air and over every living creature that
moves on the ground"* (Genesis 1:28).

This was a vital part of God's creation plan to give Adam full authority on the earth. He was given authority to bring the fullness of
the Kingdom to bear on the earth. Even at this stage there were indications in the things that God said that there was an enemy who

would have to be ruled. Genesis 2:15 (ASV) says: *"And Jehovah God took the man, and put him into the garden of Eden to dress it and to keep it;"* to rule, subdue and to increase the garden into the areas beyond.

The command to keep the garden literally means to *hedge about, guard, and protect.* Adam and Eve were given the responsibility to be the hedge, the guard, and the protection in the garden. I wonder if Adam asked God who the enemy was and what the enemy might look like! If there was no enemy then he would not have needed to do this.

The Battle in Heaven

We get a clear idea of what had happened in the heavenly realms and was now affecting earth:

> *And there was war in heaven: Michael and his angels going forth to war with the dragon; and the dragon warred and his angels; and they prevailed not, neither was their place found any more in heaven. And the great dragon was cast down, the old serpent, he that is called the Devil and Satan, the deceiver of the whole world; he was cast down to the earth, and his angels were cast down with him* (Revelation 12:7-9 ASV).

We see that there was a great battle that took place in Heaven between Michael and his angels and the great dragon (also called the serpent, the devil, and satan) and his angels. The result of this battle was a clear-out of Heaven; and the serpent and his angels (demons) were cast to the earth. As soon as the heart of satan turned against God he had to be thrown out of Heaven. Satan could not win the battle in Heaven against the other angels. This gives us an idea of the strength of God's angels. The battle may have been won in Heaven but for the job to be complete, mankind now had to face a similar battle on earth. Adam and Eve had the responsibility to rule on earth, they were given everything that they needed to do the task. Adam and Eve were able to ask their heavenly Father for any help and wisdom they needed to fulfil this task and God could even send angelic help to secure victory on earth.

We get another indicator that Adam and Eve and their descendents have a battle to win. At the beginning of Genesis 2 we read that the creation of heaven and earth was complete. The American

Standard Version of the Bible says: *"And the heavens and the earth were finished, and all the host of them"* (Gen. 2:1).

The word *host* here comes from the Hebrew root that speaks of a mass of people organized for a campaign of war. As we have seen, the war in the heavenly realm had already been won by God's angels; now there was another battle that had to be won by mankind on earth. To win this battle mankind would not only need to learn how to exercise all his own authority but also engage with the full forces of Heaven.

The Perfect Garden

In the second account of the creation of Heaven and earth, we get some glimpses of the closeness of Heaven and earth and how God intended things to be from the beginning. God planted a garden that was called Eden. It must have been an incredible place in which to live. The full excitement of Heaven and earth were combined and overlapping. The garden was called a pleasant place that was fenced around. God had made a bit of Heaven on earth. He is the ultimate garden designer, causing everything to be in the perfect location. Everything would have grown in just the right place, the trees, the shrubs, and the flowers appeared in just the right place. There would have been none of the effects of invasive weeds that we see today.

Creation was in perfect balance. The trees grew without the devastating effects of bugs and diseases. The cleanness and beauty of the spring was a constant reality. At this point the genetic diversity that produces the current range of agricultural and garden plants would have been hidden waiting to be revealed at a later date. The destruction that man has imposed on creation was not yet evident. Plants made no attempt to escape their planned place and become weeds in another spot. The glory of the Father was revealed through His creation, and there were many layers of hidden glory for mankind to enjoy.

There are a number of similarities between creation and the words Jesus spoke as He was preparing His disciples for His departure. He spoke of His Father's house and said that it was a place with many mansions and He was going there to prepare a place for each of us. These mansions were later mentioned in the same chapter referring to our bodies and that the Father was going to come and make a home in them (John 14).

The Garden of Eden was a place prepared by God specifically for mankind to dwell. It was to be a pleasant and peaceful place fenced off from the enemy. God Himself was also going to be there walking around enjoying His creation. This is evident even after the Fall when we read about God walking in the Garden in the cool of the day. When God planted the garden He made sure the trees were good to look at and the fruit good to eat. We also see that God planted the tree of life and the tree of the knowledge of good and evil in the protected garden. It is difficult for us to understand the perfect beauty of God's creation—it far exceeded the best and most beautiful place that any of us have ever seen. There was nothing that had become extinct. It was the world at its best.

A Glimpse of My Room

At one point in my journey I asked God to show me what the place was like that He prepared for me. I wanted a glimpse of Heaven. Thereafter during times of worship I found myself being distracted repeatedly by a picture of a beech woodland dressed in fresh lime green leaves with swards of beautiful bluebells waving in the breeze announcing an early spring. As I looked the other way over a fence I could see golden harvest fields running next to a country path waiting for the reaper.

When I asked God if this repeated picture was relevant, the Holy Spirit told me that this is my place. I was overwhelmed as it included my favorite scenes all in one glimpse. It was as if this was my piece of the Garden: an insight into what God had intended. It was many months later when I was describing the scene that I realized that the seasons were all mixed together: the bluebells of early spring, the fresh summer leaves of the beech, the early autumn fields ready for harvest. It is a promise of the Kingdom that the reaper will overtake the sower and the seasons will run into each other.

Why not take a few minutes now and think of the places in creation that are pleasant to you. This is your glimpse into the perfection and mystery of unspoiled creation. Many things would have been different at creation—species of animals that we might never see because they are camouflaged. How would they look without the need to remain hidden? What would the hedgehog be like without its need for protective spines? The harmony of the lion and the lamb mentioned in the Scripture was a reality. Can you imagine going into your garden and the animals and birds not fleeing in fear? These things are just some of the consequences of the Fall. The difference between God's creation before and after the Fall is unimaginable for our finite minds.

God provided a river that watered the garden and then flowed out beyond the boundary. The garden river's water was the source of life to the earth, as it divided and ran throughout the land. Even now we get only a glimpse of how many other amazing things God had hidden in His creation for mankind to discover as he increased his dominion and rule—gold, fragrances, diamonds, as well as other precious stones—all reflections of the wonders and glory of God.

What's Your Name?

While Adam was looking for a wife, God brought all the animals and birds to him to name. This was an important step in the process of ruling in creation. By naming the animals he was clearly assuming his authority over them. During this time the dragon that had been thrown out of Heaven must also have been brought to him. He was the snake with legs, the unnamed serpent. Mankind was demonstrating the authority that had been given over satan by giving him a name. During this first encounter with all the animals Adam would have been aware of their character. He would have recognized the devious nature of the serpent and realized that he was not wanted or needed within the garden. God was with Adam and he could have easily asked for more wisdom to help him if he was in any doubt. Adam's prime role in guarding the garden was not to protect against any particular species but to be aware of anything that was against the plans and purposes of God.

What Else Could They See?

The scene had been set, many things unseen by the natural eye were visible to Adam and Eve. They saw the tree of life, they saw the tree of the knowledge of good and evil, they saw the serpent. They saw their enemy coming and therefore guarded effectively against him. Imagine what it would be like for us if we could see demons in the same way we can see a spider. If we saw one perched on someone's shoulder we would just brush it off and stamp on it! Even though we cannot normally see demons with our natural eyes the same reaction should apply.

We see at the end of the Book of Revelation that the tree of life is still visible in the heavenly places. We can see the effects of satan and are told he is still wandering around looking for those he can devour. Just because some of these things are not visible to the natural eye does not mean they have disappeared. If we lock our faith into God's original plan then we have a basis for believing that God wants to restore our spiritual sight today so we can see more and more into the realms of Heaven and the angelic.

Through the Scriptures God has given us starting places to access these unseen realms. As we read and meditate on the Scriptures we give our minds fuel to understand and interpret the things that are not seen.

Satan Seizes his Opportunity

Satan is quick to make the most of early opportunities. At this stage his activities are obvious to Adam and Eve; after all, they see him with their natural eyes! He approaches Eve and starts the process to disarm her and focus her attention away from God. The responsibility given to Adam and Eve would have enabled them to see immediately that the serpent should not be in the garden, he was disturbing the peace. This was their opportunity to demonstrate that they were not only keeping the Garden in order but also guarding it against unwanted intruders.

In the middle of the garden is the tree that is pleasing to the eye, good for food and desirable for gaining wisdom. It is similar to all the other trees except that it can give wisdom. Satan points out that even though they have been told not to eat from the tree, if they do their eyes will be opened and they will be able to distinguish between good and evil just like God. While satan is speaking about eyes opening, the real truth was exactly the opposite—their eyes would be closed from the spiritual realm because of sin and their disobedience.

God had given Adam instruction about the tree; he knew that the consequence of eating from this tree was death. Eve was also aware of the instruction and consequence. God did not want mankind to be short on wisdom but had made man dependent on Him and a relationship with Him to gain wisdom. Any wisdom that was released from eating the tree's fruit would be earthly wisdom tainted by sin. The wisdom that comes from God is pure in every way and will bring us into a place of purity as we act on it.

Eve, instead, followed the instructions of satan and the consequence of that disobedience is the dominant controlling aspect of the world's fallen state today. It is true that Adam and Eve's eyes were opened and they could instantly see. They looked at each other saw their nakedness and they made desperate attempts to hide. Sin had an immediate corrupting effect. At this point, though, they were still able to see the things of the heavenly realm around them.

God is God

God came to Adam and Eve, as usual, in the cool of the day. They were ashamed and tried to hide themselves. But the effect of sin did not cause God to withdraw from them—they withdrew from God. God banished Adam and Eve from the Garden because of their disobedience and He placed cherubim by the entrance to guard it. As a result of sin we cannot see the cherubim, or see into the spiritual world through our natural eyes. God wants to teach us how see these realms through the eyes of our hearts. The perfect order that God planned for earth changed with Adam and Eve. They were given the mandate to rule on earth under the guiding hand of God but they dishonored Him by disobeying His instructions.

The rule on earth was been handed over to satan. He is the prince of the air, with the right to rule and continuously increase the distortion of sin in the hearts of man.

Chapter 6

THE THRONE ROOM AND GLORY

Cherubim

The cherubim have been placed by God at the entrance to the Garden. They have the responsibility to guard the way into the Garden and to guard/hedge the way to the tree of life.

> *So he drove out the man; and he placed at the east of the garden of Eden the **Cherubim**, and the flame of a sword which turned every way, to keep the way of the tree of life* (Genesis 3:24 ASV emphasis added).

The cherubim are mentioned numerous times in the Old Testament and they have a key role in the heavenly realms. There is only one direct mention of them in the New Testament where they are called the cherubim of glory.

Above the ark were the cherubim of the Glory, overshadowing the atonement cover. But we cannot discuss these things in detail now (Hebrews 9:5).

This is one of the verses that I wish in some ways had not been written. It's frustrating that they did not go into more detail. On the other hand we have to see what the Holy Spirit wants to communicate. I believe God is very simply telling us that there is so much more He wants to reveal though His Holy Spirit, through dreams, visions, and heavenly encounters. If we stop at what is already explained clearly then we will miss out on the depths of life in God.

Around the Glory Zone

When God created Adam and Eve and placed them in the Garden, His intention was for this to be the place where the glory of God was found. The cherubim are found around the place of glory, the weighty place of the presence of God. One of the key roles given to the cherubim was to guard the way to the place of glory, the place where God Himself dwelt. But Adam and Eve were forced out of the Garden; they were no longer permitted to live in the place of the glory of God. Where they had been clothed in His glory before they had sinned, they now saw their nakedness. They had given up part of their mandate to see the earth filled with the knowledge of God's glory. Even though they had been forced out of the glory realm they were still experiencing the presence of God. It was not until Cain murdered his brother Abel that we are told that man was driven out of the presence of God (see Gen. 4:13-16). The cherubim were the guards to the realm of glory, up to this point they must have been around the Garden because they are found where the glory of God is found.

Cherubim and the Tabernacle

The next time the cherubim are mentioned is when God gives Moses the instructions to build the tabernacle. It is an important point to remember that God was providing Moses instructions based on what already existed in the heavenly realms. The tabernacle, and later the temple, were visible reminders of the heavens. We are told in Hebrews:

> *They serve at a sanctuary that is a copy and shadow of what is in heaven. This is why Moses was warned when he was about to build the tabernacle: "See to it that you make everything according to the pattern shown you on the mountain"* (Hebrews 8:5).

God commanded Moses to make the Tabernacle so that we would have a place of meeting–a place where His weighty glory could be manifest again on earth. This is seen as soon as the Tabernacle is set up and dedicated.

> *Then the cloud covered the Tent of Meeting, and the glory of the Lord filled the tabernacle. Moses could not enter the Tent of Meeting because the cloud had settled upon it, and the glory of the Lord filled the tabernacle* (Exodus 40:34-35).

Moses is told to make two cherubim that will be above the mercy seat. He is given the exact design. Their position reflects their position in the Garden and we see they have a key role in the place of the glory.

> *Make an atonement cover of pure gold–two and a half cubits long and a cubit and a half wide. And make two cherubim out of hammered gold at the ends of the cover. Make one cherub on one end and the second cherub on the other; make the cherubim of one piece with the cover, at the two ends. The cherubim are to have their wings spread upward, overshadowing the cover with them. The cherubim are to face each other, looking toward the cover. Place the cover on top of the ark and put in the ark the Testimony, which I will give you. There, above the cover between the two cherubim that are over the ark of the Testimony, I will meet with you and give you all My commands for the Israelites* (Exodus 25:17-22).

Later we see when Moses came to speak with the Lord that He would speak from above the cherubim.

> *When Moses entered the Tent of Meeting to speak with the Lord, he heard the voice speaking to him from between the two cherubim above the atonement cover on the ark of the Testimony. And he spoke with Him* (Numbers 7:89).

In the same way that the cherubim guard the way into the glory they guard the way into the glory of God when He appears on earth. We see a number of other times when God demonstrates the position of the cherubim. They are sewn into the curtain that separates the Holy place from the Most Holy place. Again this is a position of guarding the access into the glory realm of God.

The cherubim continue to have their place when the temple is built. They were made to cover again in the inner sanctuary. They were made of olive wood and overlaid with gold. The walls of the temple were covered with cherubim, palm trees, and open flowers. They were again overlaid with gold. It is a constant reminder that where the glory of God is, the cherubim are.

Carrying the Glory

The cherubim are the carriers of the glory presence of God. There are many similarities here to the responsibility given to the Levites to carry the Ark of the presence of God, and the fact that now the believers are the carriers of the presence of God with the Holy Spirit inside them.

> He mounted the cherubim and flew; He soared on the wings of the wind (Psalm 18:10).

The most dramatic revelations about the cherubim and their role and responsibility come when Ezekiel has his amazing visions of Heaven. Where the glory of God is seen, the cherubim are involved.

In Ezekiel 1 the prophet is by the river Kebar when the heavens are opened to him and he has visions of the heavenly realm. He speaks of the living creatures. Later in Ezekiel he speaks of the cherubim:

> Then the cherubim rose upward. These were the living creatures I had seen by the Kebar River (Ezekiel 10:15).

Ezekiel Explains

Ezekiel saw an opening of the realms of the spirit that had been closed as a result of Adam and Eve's sin. As we look at Ezekiel's description we see that on numerous occasions he used the phrase "the likeness":

> *I looked, and I saw* **the likeness** *of a throne of sapphire above the expanse that was over the heads of the cherubim* (Ezekiel 10:1 emphasis added).

He was seeing heavenly things and then he was trying to describe them in human language. This was not an easy task and is certainly not easy to understand. We will never fully understand the mysteries of the glory of God. The Scriptures say those who speak in tongues will be speaking the language of men and of angels. It appears that there are angelic languages needed to speak of many of the heavenly things.

Why not spend a little time reading the Ezekiel chapters 1 and 10. Do not try and understand everything but take time to absorb this realm of glory. Every day for about one month the Holy Spirit prompted me to read Ezekiel 1. At the time I was not sure what understanding I gained but I did find that I had an increased revelation of the glory realms of God.

Other Points of Glory

Ezekiel's visions of the glory of God coming (Ezekiel 1) have more than passing comparisons with the events on the day of Pentecost. Ezekiel saw a violent wind, cloud, and flashes of lightning in his visions. The signs on the day of Pentecost included the sound of a violent wind, and tongues of fire resting on each person. It was a day when the glory of God came.

At the end of Ezekiel 1 he says that all he has seen is the appearance of the likeness of the glory of God. He describes how the cherubim are the carriers of the glory of God as well as the heavenly guardians. We get an indication here of how God has set up His kingdom to work on earth. The believer is the carrier of the glory and the angels are sent to minister to and guard the saints. They are reflecting the role of the cherubim in Heaven.

Although nothing is said about their role in the New Testament, major change must have taken place. They no longer needed to provide the total guard as Jesus became the way for us to come to the

Father. When Jesus came to earth, Heaven opened and has stayed open for us through Him. As Jesus Himself said, *"I am the way and the truth and the life. No one comes to the Father except through Me"* (John 14:6). The cherubim are clearly still linked to the glory realm. They were probably involved on the day of Pentecost and every time the manifest glory of God is seen.

Seraphim

Isaiah's eyes were opened to the seraphim around the throne of God—they are very unusual creatures with six wings, two covering their faces, two covering their feet, and the other ones used to fly (see Isaiah 6).

Seraphims minister very powerfully around the throne calling out to each other. Their voices shake Heaven and release the glory of God. They also appear to have a role in releasing the forgiveness of God. One took a coal from the altar and touched the prophet's lips. It is possible they continue to release realms of glory and holiness on earth.

Chapter 7

ANGELS WITH LIMITED ACCESS

The veil between the heavenly realms was now in place. The effect of sin meant that mankind was no longer able to see through the veil. This does not mean there was no further angelic activity, though. The angels had a limited impact on earth in Old Testament times.

Enoch

Hidden in the middle of what appears to be a routine genealogy there is an indication that the plans of God have not changed toward mankind. We come across a slightly mysterious man who in the midst of ungodliness was living a different life. Enoch walked with God for over 300 years and then there came the day when God took him away (Gen. 5:21-24). Even his body was taken through to eternity. This is a demonstration that the veil that seemed to be closed, guarded by cherubim, was still open to those who would "walk with God" by faith.

In the Old Testament there are dozens of references to angels and the writings of the Psalmists are especially very insightful.

Angelic Protection

Before David became king he was on the run from King Saul. He wrote Psalm 34 when he knew what it was like to be under pressure in every way. Even in this situation, though, he knew how to give thanks and praise because he realized God saved him. He writes: "*The angel of the Lord encamps around those who fear him, and he delivers them*" (Psalm 34:7).

We have an angelic bodyguard working on our behalf. This is an amazing realization—God sets His angels around us. As we walk in fear of Him He will protect us and even deliver us from dangerous situations. Later in the book you will read about modern day stories of the saving power of God through His angels.

This theme of the protection of the angels continues in Psalms:

If you make the Most High your dwelling—
even the Lord, who is my refuge—
then no harm will befall you,
no disaster will come near your tent.
For He will command His angels concerning you
to guard you in all your ways;
they will lift you up in their hands,
so that you will not strike your foot against a stone.
You will tread upon the lion and the cobra;
you will trample the great lion and the serpent (Psalm 91:9-13).

As we focus on God we receive an amazing benefit. God is committed to working with us with His angels. We see in the Old Testament the original plan from the Garden of Eden being activated.

Angels Revealed

David clearly has a good understanding of the work of the angelic. In one of my favorite Psalms he reminds us of all the benefits that we have received from the Lord. He speaks of His compassionate heart and abounding love. At the end of the Psalm he says:

Praise the Lord, you His angels, you mighty ones who do His bidding, who obey His word. Praise the Lord, all His heavenly hosts, you His servants who do His will (Psalm 103:20-21).

The angels are involved in praise, they do whatever the Lord commands as well as continually obeying His word. Now we look at a few specific Old Testament angelic encounters.

Hagar and Ishmael
(Genesis 16 and Genesis 21)

The first reference to angels in the Bible is when one visits Hagar. She ran away from home because she was badly treated by her mistress Sarah, Abraham's wife. Hagar was sitting near a spring in the desert and an angel was sent out to find her. It must have been quite a shock to Hagar when the angel neared and spoke to her by name, and told her the name of her mistress as well. This is not the sort of thing you would expect to happen when you are alone in a desert.

Hagar's experience reveals much about the heart of God. He will always search us out—no matter where we are. Jesus speaks of this same desire of God in the parables when He shares about the lost coin and the lost sheep (Luke 15:8-10; Matt. 18:10-14). God always brings us to a place with Him where we belong. The angel that searched for Hagar knew who she was. This is the heart of God for us too—He knows us by name. We find out elsewhere in the Bible that our names and dwelling place are known in the heavenly realms.

One of my prayers is that I am not just known by the angels in Heaven but the demons have also heard about me. We are told in Acts 19 that the demons know about Jesus. When Jewish priests try to drive out an evil spirit in the name of the Jesus, whom Paul preaches, the demon tells them he knows about Jesus and Paul—but not them. We are His children and we cause damage to the kingdom of darkness because we are known there and have a reputation! This is our birthright.

The angel that visited Hagar brings a very clear word from God including naming her child Ishmael. The name Ishmael means *God will hear.* Hagar's reaction to this revelation is to declare the name of the well she is sitting next to Beer Lahai Roi, which means *the well of the living one who sees.* The effect of this visitation of an angel is dramatic. It changes the life and direction that Hagar is taking, and it also sets the direction for the next generation. This is a principle that works throughout Scripture—every encounter with Heaven leaves an eternal deposit.

Hagar had another angelic visitation a few years later after the birth of Sarah's son, Isaac. Sarah did not want Hagar or Ishmael near her family. She ordered Abraham to send them away (Gen. 21:8-20). Abraham provided her with food and water and she wandered out into the desert with her son. It was not long before the water was gone and she sat down prepared to die. We are told that God heard the boy crying from Heaven. This time the angel spoke to her from Heaven and repeated the promises of God to the child. Then a miracle takes place.

> *Then God opened her eyes and she saw a well of water. So she went and filled the skin with water and gave the boy a drink* (Genesis 21:19).

Ishmael continued to live in the desert and there he grew up. This angelic encounter changed a hostile environment into a place where it was possible for him to live. The principle for us is simple; it is only by the grace of God that our eyes will be open to see anything in the heavenly realm. It has nothing to do with how our life is going at that time. It is easy to think that we will become more aware of the angelic if everything is going well, but this is certainly not the case for Hagar and Ishmael.

Abraham and Angels

God repeatedly sends his angels to Abraham. They speak about many things including blessing and increase. It is an angel that spoke to Abraham as he prepared to sacrifice his son on an altar (Gen. 22:1-11). The word of God came and Abraham's life was changed forever—one of Abraham's defining moments. Later in his life Abraham is confident that an angel would lead the search for his son's wife (Gen. 24:7). It is interesting to note that angels come to earth and speak, as well as speak directly from Heaven. The veil that is in place for mankind does not restrict the angelic realm.

Jacob's Dream

This is a very familiar story and any look at the angelic realm has to include this dream. One thing that I love about this dream is the timing. Jacob is simply out on a journey from one place to another. The place where he stops is initially referred to as "a certain place." He only stops there because the sun has set and he wants to settle down to sleep. This type of situation is true of many encounters with God. We have not planned anything, we are simply going about our business and God decides that there is a special divine encounter coming our way. Jacob lays down his head to get some sleep when he has a dream. In this dream he sees a ladder with its feet on earth and its top in heaven. He sees the angels ascending and descending on the ladder. The Lord is at the top of the ladder; He tells Jacob that the land he is sleeping on has been given to him and to his offspring. God promises that He will look after Jacob on his journey and Jacob's reaction when he wakes up is to make some declarations.

> *"Surely the Lord is in this place, and I was not aware of it." He was afraid and said, "How awesome is this place! This is none other than the house of God; this is the gate of heaven"* (Genesis 28:16-17).

God likes surprises and sometimes will do things in a way that gets our full attention. This dream was a moment when God was revealing the destiny of Jacob and his family. Jacob takes what the Lord has spoken and promises to give God a tithe of everything when he has completed his journey and has seen that God is watching over him. We also see that this encounter uncovers the destiny of the city. The place that was originally only called "a certain place" suddenly becomes significant. Before Jacob leaves the place he changes the name of the city from Luz to Bethel.

Jacob's dream reveals a number of things about the heavenly realm at this time. The Lord is at the top of the ladder and the angels are acting as the intermediaries, bringing heavenly messages to earth. Their place of access is through the place called the *house of God* or the *gateway*. The original name of the city was Luz; which comes from the root meaning *nut tree*, maybe the almond. The almond tree is significant in Bible times as it is the tree that shows the first sign of spring. It was the *watching tree,* announcing the change of season. Luz was a place that was watching for a heavenly revelation. When the revelation came, Jacob renamed the city because now it was a *gateway to Heaven, the house of God*—a taste of what is to come.

Jesus refers to the same passage with a fresh slant in the New Testament, *"I tell you the truth, you shall see heaven open, and the angels of God ascending and descending on the Son of Man"* (John 1:51).

There are a number of different things that can be drawn from this passage. I think that all of them are relevant to us.

Jesus is indicating that He is the ladder to Heaven and now the angels ascend and descend on Him. In John's gospel He puts this in a more familiar form when he says *"I am the way."*

Jesus is also indicating that the angels are no longer moving up and down on a place (Luz/Bethel) they are ascending and descending on the Son of Man. Jesus says that this will be one of the great revelations that the disciple Nathaniel will see. Jesus comes to bring the first sign of spring like the almond tree. He is waiting to bring the revelation that the house of God is on earth! As we follow this through we realize we are now God's sons on earth; angelic activity is focused around us.

This was not the only dream in which an angel appeared to Jacob. It was an angel that told him to leave Laban's house and return to his native land. (See Genesis 31.)

Moses and the Angels

In the Old Testament angels are very involved in bringing the purposes of God to earth. We see in the life of Moses and the Israelites angels play a key role. Moses spent 40 years isolated from his people when an angel appeared to him. While Moses was out with the sheep at Horeb an angel appeared to him in the flames of a burning bush. Moses is commissioned to be the deliverer of Israel. There are two significant references to the role of the angelic during the ministry of Moses.

The first is found when the Israelites escaped from Egypt.

Then the angel of God, who had been traveling in front of Israel's army, withdrew and went behind them... (Exodus 14:19).

78

*See, I am sending an angel ahead of you to guard you along the way
and to bring you to the place I have prepared. Pay attention to him
and listen to what he says. Do not rebel against him; he will not forgive your rebellion, since My Name is in him. If you listen carefully
to what he says and do all that I say, I will be an enemy to your enemies and will oppose those who oppose you. My angel will go
ahead of you and bring you into the land of the Amorites, Hittites,
Perizzites, Canaanites, Hivites and Jebusites, and I will wipe them
out* (Exodus 23:20-23).

It is easy for us to look at these two passages and think how amazing it was to be led so clearly by angels. The angel showed them the
way to go; he guarded them on the way. The angel had responsibility
to lead them to the land that had been prepared for them. If they paid
attention and listened to him then their enemies would be destroyed.

But we need to remember that the role of angels has changed and
God has an even greater plan for us. He sent the Holy Spirit to *dwell
in* us; God Himself lives in us by His Spirit. This is even more amazing than any angelic visitation. The Holy Spirit brings believers into
all truth. Jesus Himself is preparing a place for us and He promises
to come back and take us to be with Him (John 14).

The angels continue to play an important role as they help those
who have inherited salvation. The angels are the ones in the Old Testament who are given the responsibility to help the Israelites. As we
saw in the dream of Jacob, they brought heaven's commands to earth.

The second key role of the angels that was initiated during the life
of Moses is best expressed in Galatians:

*What, then, was the purpose of the law? It was added because of
transgressions until the Seed to whom the promise referred had
come. The law was put into effect through angels by a mediator. A
mediator, however, does not represent just one party; but God is one*
(Galatians 3:19-20).

In an earlier chapter we saw what happened to the angels when
Adam and Eve were thrown out of the Garden. They became the
guards that kept mankind separated from the glory realm. When the
law was given it was the angels that were around the throne and

79

brought it to Moses on earth. The angels had a key role in bringing heavenly things to earth.

Balaam and the Speaking Donkey

Balaam was a prophet with a reputation. The King of Moab, who was fighting against the Israelites, recognized that those Balaam blessed were blessed and those he cursed were cursed. The King sent some of his men to Balaam to pay him money to prophesy a curse over the people of God. We get the best insight into Balaam from a reference in the New Testament when his life is used as a warning to others.

> *They have left the straight way and wandered off to follow the way of Balaam son of Beor, who loved the wages of wickedness. But he was rebuked for his wrongdoing by a donkey—a beast without speech—who spoke with a man's voice and restrained the prophet's madness* (2 Peter 2:15-16).

Balaam was tempted to go away from God and help the enemy of God's people. We are also told that he showed the King of Moab how to lead the people of God into idolatry and sexual immorality (Rev. 2:14). It was this liaison that eventually led to his death (Num. 31:8).

Even though God told him not to go with the King of Moab, Balaam kept going back to God and asking the questions again because of the wickedness that was in his heart. What follows next is one of the more unusual accounts in the Scriptures.

Balaam heads out with the princes of Moab, and God sends an angel to stop him. Balaam's eyes were not open to see the angel but the donkey did! The donkey kept reacting to the angel even though Balaam beat her. Eventually the donkey just sat down. This is a clear lesson for us, just because we cannot see angels does not mean they are not there. It is very easy for us to take this attitude about the angelic and become skeptical of the things others see. I remember another time when I had a car accident; I did not see the other vehicle until I hit it. The fact I did not see it did not mean it was not there—a costly mistake! We need to keep our hearts and minds open. I love what happens next in this story.

> *When the donkey saw the angel of the Lord, she lay down under Bal-*
> *aam, and he was angry and beat her with his staff. Then the Lord*
> *opened the donkey's mouth, and she said to Balaam, "What have I*
> *done to you to make you beat me these three times?" Balaam answered*
> *the donkey, "You have made a fool of me! If I had a sword in my*
> *hand, I would kill you right now"* (Numbers 22:27-29).

Apart from being an insight into donkey behavior we see that Bal-aam is so caught up in his wickedness that he does not see the angel but he immediately replies to the rebuke of a donkey and threatens to kill him. The conversation goes on, Balaam blinded by his anger. God has one other way to get Balaam's full attention.

> *Then the Lord opened Balaam's eyes, and he saw the angel of the*
> *Lord standing in the road with his sword drawn. So he bowed low*
> *and fell facedown* (Numbers 22:31).

Balaam is totally caught up with himself yet God decides to open his eyes to see. At this point Balaam realizes that it's not the donkey that is facing death but *he* is facing death. His life is saved by the speaking donkey. Later in the book we will learn how to discern an-gelic activity—remembering that it is only by the grace of God that our eyes are opened. It is important to realize that there is no substi-tute for straightening our lives to the path of righteousness so we do not walk in error.

An Angel?

We saw earlier how the angel spoke to Abraham from Heaven and he received the revelation that God would provide. Gideon also received a revelation of the character of God through an an-gelic visitation.

Often portrayed as a fearful person, Gideon was hiding away threshing wheat in a winepress. An angel came and sat down and started to talk to Gideon. At this point he did not realize that he was talking with an angel. The angel told him that the Lord was with him. It is clear that Gideon had already considered the situation as he talked with the angel. He could not see how the Lord could be with Israel since they were under so much oppression. In fact, it was amazing that

Gideon actually had any wheat to thresh considering the enemies were destroying all the crops as soon as they were planted. Before the angel left, Gideon wanted to make an offering.

> *The angel of God said to him, "Take the meat and the unleavened bread, place them on this rock, and pour out the broth." And Gideon did so. With the tip of the staff that was in his hand, the angel of the Lord touched the meat and the unleavened bread. Fire flared from the rock, consuming the meat and the bread. And the angel of the Lord disappeared. When Gideon realized that it was the angel of the Lord, he exclaimed, "Ah, Sovereign Lord! I have seen the angel of the Lord face to face!"* (Judges 6:20-22)

He must have wondered what happened right in front of his eyes. He didn't realize he was talking to an angel and now he was fearful for his life. God speaks to him and tells him that he will not die. Gideon builds an altar and declares that, "The Lord is Peace." This is another example of the revelation that comes from an angelic encounter. This is only a shadow of the revelation that God brings to believers through the Holy Spirit.

Samson is Here

The birth of Samson was declared to his parents by an angel. When the angel first appeared to his mother she was not sure about his origin. The angel told her that although she was previously unable to have children she was going to have a son who was to be set apart as a Nazarite (Judges 13). Samson's mother told her husband that the man she had spoken to had been awesome "like an angel." Her husband prayed that the word would be confirmed to him. God sent the angel again and it is clear that the husband did not realize he was talking to an angel. He probably thought he was speaking to one of the amazing prophets. It was only when they made a sacrifice and the angel went up in the flame, that they realized that an angel spoke to them about the birth of their son.

An Angel Visits Elijah

In this account we see that any encounter with the angelic is by grace. Elijah was not in a place of being totally fired up and serving

God when this encounter happened. He was full of fear, running away from Jezebel (see 1 Kings 19). In fact, Elijah had come to the end of his strength and asked God to take his life—he did not even value himself. Then he fell asleep in total exhaustion. It is amazing to see the effect of the encounter that follows.

The angel gives Elijah a nudge to wake him up. He tells him to get up and eat. Elijah looks around, sees the food and drinks, takes his fill, and falls back to sleep. This little episode makes me think that we may actually react very differently to a visible angel than we might predict. The angel returns a second time to Elijah and the effects are spectacular.

> *The angel of the Lord came back a second time and touched him and said, "Get up and eat, for the journey is too much for you." So he got up and ate and drank. Strengthened by that food, he traveled forty days and forty nights until he reached Horeb, the mountain of God. There he went into a cave and spent the night* (1 Kings 19:7-9).

He obeys the angel and then finds that he has enough strength to travel for 40 days and nights. It seems that the visit of the angel is secondary to Elijah who is still stuck in a very lonely way of thinking. I think there may be times when the visit of an angel seems so normal that we do not realize what is happening. Maybe we would simply be distracted by the angel and ask too many questions if we were fully aware.

David and the Census

King David had a census taken of the Israelites. This is something that greatly displeased God. David repented, but God sent Gad to bring the word of God. Gad is described as David's seer (1 Chron. 21:9). The Bible makes a distinction between the prophets and those that could see through visions what God was doing.

Gad gave David a number of options as a judgment for his wrongdoing. An angel was sent to execute the plague on earth. We are told 70,000 people were killed before the Lord commanded the angel to stop at the threshing floor of Araunah the Jebusite. The meaning of Araunah was *strength*. It was as if David's strength had to be broken and he had to come to a true place of repentance to bring an end to this disaster.

> *David looked up and saw the angel of the Lord standing between heaven and earth, with a drawn sword in his hand extended over Jerusalem. Then David and the elders, clothed in sackcloth, fell face-down* (1 Chronicles 21:16).

This angel had brought the purposes of God on earth, even though it does not fit our normal thoughts on the activities of angels.

Angels in the Book of Daniel

The life of Daniel was marked by the unusual and the miraculous. Early in his life he refused to compromise his walk with God even in the face of death. His friends walked with the same determination when they were thrown into the fiery furnace. They managed to survive the excessive heat without even a hint of smoke on them. King Nebuchadnezzar concluded that an angel must have protected them (Dan. 3:28). This story must have been the talking point of the nation at the time.

A bit later Daniel faced another command to compromise his faith when King Darius made a decree. Anyone who worshiped anyone other than King Darius would be thrown into the lion's den. Daniel did not bend under pressure but continued to pray in exactly the same way. The king's advisors were determined to make the king carry out his decree. The king realized that he had to put Daniel into the lion's den and makes this interesting statement as he seals door: *"Thy God whom thou servest continually, He will deliver thee."* (Daniel 6:16 ASV).

The king is so deeply troubled that he can not sleep that night. He is clearly hoping for a miracle as he goes to check the den first thing in the morning. He wants to know if Daniel's God was big enough to rescue him. He must have been shocked when Daniel replied:

> *"O king, live forever! My God sent his angel, and he shut the mouths of the lions. They have not hurt me, because I was found innocent in His sight. Nor have I ever done any wrong before you, O king"* (Daniel 6:21-22).

I wonder if Daniel could see the angel that had closed the mouths of the lions. If he could it must have been very amusing to watch. Any fear that Daniel may have had would have changed into laughter as he waited for the king to open the den door in the morning. The lions must have been hungry as they immediately crushed Daniel's accusers when they were thrown into the den. I believe that the angels continue to work on behalf of the sons of God, bringing deliverance and saving lives many more times than we are aware.

Daniel has a number of different angelic visitations including one from Gabriel who he calls a man but who also flew to him (Dan. 9:21). The only other mentions of Gabriel are when he announces the birth of John the Baptist and later Jesus. In both cases the angel came to bring instruction and understanding. One other angelic encounter that Daniel experienced gives us clues to the way the heavenly realms work. We will look at this encounter in the next chapter before delving into the angelic involvement in the life of Jesus.

Chapter 8

HEAVEN AND EARTH

It is clear from a number of different references in the Bible that there is a structure in the heavens. This should be of no surprise to us, as we notice on earth many authority structures from government, to workplace, home, and in creation itself. The earth reflects the heavens. A good authority structure helps things run well. God Himself is the highest authority in all things. In our study of the angelic and heavenly realms an understanding of this structure will help us.

It was early in my working life that I came to appreciate the importance of understanding my position and the authority given to that position. I had just assumed my first supervisory role and was struggling to adjust to the new responsibility of giving clear direction to those who worked for me. One day an employee turned to me and, in a rather frustrated voice, said, "Listen, your job is to tell me what to do and my job is to do it." I was rather startled by his outburst but knew he was right and I had to change my approach. I had been given the authority to make certain decisions so I needed to go ahead and make them.

Jesus commented on this very thing when a centurion came to Him at Capernaum. He came asking for help because his servant was at home paralyzed. When Jesus said He would go and heal the man, the centurion said:

> *"Lord, I do not deserve to have You come under my roof. But just say the word, and my servant will be healed. For I myself am a man under authority, with soldiers under me. I tell this one, 'Go,' and he goes; and that one, 'Come,' and he comes. I say to my servant, 'Do this,' and he does it." When Jesus heard this, He was astonished and said to those following Him, "I tell you the truth, I have not found anyone in Israel with such great faith..."* (Matthew 8:8-10).

When we understand the authority structure in Heaven and on earth and our position we will understand our authority over sickness, how to minister and pray, how to deal with anything demonic, as well as our relationship with angels.

The NIV Bible has a section titled *"The Supremacy of Christ"* that introduces the heavenly realms. Here is an introduction to the heavenly realms.

> *He is the image of the invisible God, the firstborn over all creation. For by him all things were created: things in heaven and on earth, visible and invisible, whether thrones or powers or rulers or authorities; all things were created by him and for him. He is before all things, and in him all things hold together. And he is the head of the body, the church; he is the beginning and the firstborn from among the dead, so that in everything he might have the supremacy. For God was pleased to have all his fullness dwell in him, and through him to reconcile to himself all things, whether things on earth or things in heaven, by making peace through his blood, shed on the cross* (Colossians 1:15-20).

God's original plan was that everything that was created was created for and by Christ. It is clear that even satan was originally created for Christ. This passage shows that even when man sinned and went away from God that Christ became the source of reconciliation and peace.

The importance of understanding a little of this realm is emphasized in Ephesians 6:12: *"For our struggle is not against flesh and blood, but against the rulers, against the authorities, against the powers of this dark world and against the spiritual forces of evil in the heavenly realms."*

In Hebrews we get a summary of the situation in the heavenly realm and what Jesus did. We shall look at this scripture in some detail.

It is not to angels that He has subjected the world to come, about which we are speaking. But there is a place where someone has testified: "What is man that You are mindful of him, the son of man that You care for him? You made him a little lower than the angels; You crowned him with glory and honor and put everything under his feet." In putting everything under him, God left nothing that is not subject to him. Yet at present we do not see everything subject to him. But we see Jesus, who was made a little lower than the angels, now crowned with glory and honor because He suffered death, so that by the grace of God He might taste death for everyone (Hebrews 2:5-9).

When God created the world there was a distinct authority structure that He put into place. It is clear that all authority came from God in the first place, but He delegated His authority in different ways to the angelic beings and also to mankind.

Initially mankind was given full authority on earth. It was only God Himself who had more authority. The angels had less authority on earth than mankind. The situation did not stay according to this initial order for long. It is not clear when satan tried to gain authority. We do know that the battle took place in the heavens (Rev. 12:7). Satan was the chief worshiper, he tried to gain equality with God. Michael and his angels engaged in the battle against the dragon and his angels. Satan tried to fight back but was not strong enough and lost his place in heaven. He was hurled down to earth with his angels (demons). On earth he set out to gain control and lead the whole world astray (Rev. 12:7-10).

This was the first change in the authority structure, satan now had even less authority than Michael and his angels (Rev. 12:7-10). They had won the victory in Heaven. This left a second battle to take place on earth where God had given the authority to rule the earth to mankind.

The second change in authority happened when Adam and Eve listened to the serpent. They were told by God not to touch the fruit of the tree of the knowledge of good and evil. When they listened to satan they were already in trouble. They should have stopped him from talking and kicked him out of the Garden. He quickly wove a web of deception and laid his trap. When Adam and Eve obeyed him, instead of obeying God, they changed allegiance. They lost the authority given to them on earth. At this point they became subject to satan and his schemes to bring bondage, death, and destruction.

The change was so dramatic that even earth and creation itself was now subject to the authority of satan. We are told that earth was subject to frustration (Rom. 8:20). Paul refers to satan as the prince of the air (Eph. 2:2). At this point we can see that the angels are now in a place of higher authority than fallen man. They are set as guards over the things of Heaven. The new authority structure in simple terms was: God, angels, satan, mankind.

For the plans of God to be fulfilled, this authority structure had to be changed. The role of Jesus in this was crucial and He agreed with the plan of His Father. He took the place of ultimate humility.

> *Your attitude should be the same as that of Christ Jesus: Who, being in very nature God, did not consider equality with God something to be grasped, but made Himself nothing, taking the very nature of a servant, being made in human likeness* (Philippians 2:5-7).

Jesus could never lay aside the fact He was God, but He chose not to set aside this right. As we saw in Hebrews He became a little lower than the angels. He became like mankind. The authority structure was now beginning to change. Jesus had allowed Himself to take the lowest place *but* He was not going to be subject to satan.

He lived a life not subject to the sin that tied up man. He would win victory over satan on earth. In the next chapter we look in more detail about the steps to this victory and the involvement of the angelic. Jesus was willing to complete His Father's plan even to the point of death. He was totally dependent on His Father to provide the Holy Spirit to raise Him from the dead.

*And having disarmed the powers and authorities, He made a public
spectacle of them, triumphing over them by the cross* (Colossians 2:15).

The cross was not just about dealing with sin: It was about removing power from satan so mankind could have the opportunity to
reign and rule in life again.

At this time of authority change Jesus even took the Gospel to the
depths of the earth (1 Peter 3:19) and when He was resurrected to
life went back to Heaven. He is now crowned with glory and honor
and given the highest place of authority.

*Therefore God exalted Him to the highest place and gave Him the
name that is above every name, that at the name of Jesus every knee
should bow, in heaven and on earth and under the earth, and every
tongue confess that Jesus Christ is Lord, to the glory of God the Father* (Philippians 2:9-11).

There is a dramatic shift taking place not just on earth but to the
whole structure of heaven. In the process of His resurrection Jesus
created a way that anyone who came to Him could also be given a
new position.

*When He ascended on high, He led captives in His train and gave
gifts to men* (Ephesians 4:8).

The world dynamic has changed forever. Fallen man may still be
subject to satan and his demons, the earth may still be subject to frustrations, but the believer has a new authority. Every believer has a new
position with Christ, seated far above all other rule and authority.

*And God raised us up with Christ and seated us with Him in the
heavenly realms in Christ Jesus, in order that in the coming ages He
might show the incomparable riches of His grace, expressed in His
kindness to us in Christ Jesus* (Ephesians 2:6-8).

Because of Christ's sacrifice, the new authority structure is: God;
Jesus and His sons (the believers) seated together; the angels; satan;
and then, fallen man. When we pray, we pray from a place of authority on earth, we are able to command healing and deliver people
from demons. In other words, believers fulfill the commission given
to the disciples.

When Jesus returns, the picture will be complete. As we look at the way God has organized His creation we realize that the angels are now sent to serve those who have inherited salvation—there is no blockage into the presence of our Heavenly Father.

Chapter 9

JESUS HERALDS
A NEW ERA

When Jesus came to earth there was a time of spiritual revolution taking place. When a revolution takes place, the authority structures and ways of doing things are changed forever. We are well aware that after His resurrection the outpouring of the Holy Spirit brought about the birth of the Church. There were also many changes that happened in the heavenly realms at this time. Every piece of revelation up to this time had only been a shadow of the fullness that came in Christ.

In the past God spoke to our forefathers through the prophets at many times and in various ways, but in these last days He has spoken to us by his Son, whom He appointed heir of all things, and through whom He made the universe. The Son is the radiance of God's glory and the exact representation of His being, sustaining all things by His powerful word. After He had provided purification for sins, He sat down at the right hand of the Majesty in heaven. So He became as much superior to the angels as the name He has inherited is superior to theirs (Hebrews 1:1-4).

Before Jesus we had bits and pieces of revelation and now we have the fullness in Him. Next we will look at some of the heavenly realm shifting that happened throughout the life of Jesus.

As we have read, in the Old Testament angels had a key role in bringing the law to the people. Now they have the vital job of announcing and bringing change in divine order. There is a sudden increase of angelic activity around the time of Jesus' birth.

Although there are many things that the Father knows that have not been revealed to His angels when they come to earth they bring incredible detail in everything that they say. The angels bring the good news from Heaven of the birth of John (the Baptist) and the birth of Jesus. They appear in dreams as well as in person.

During this time, Zechariah has been selected by lot to go and burn the incense at the altar. Although this was a very important time for Zechariah it was something that had been going on for years. But this time, suddenly an angel appears to him by the altar of incense. He would have been shocked and startled as he would not have been expecting anyone to be there. The angel spoke to him by name and spoke also of his wife by name, telling him in great detail about the child who would be born to him. Zechariah is caught by his own inability to make things happen—he's just too old, and so is his wife. As a result of his unbelief he was struck dumb until his son John was born. The angel that appeared to Zechariah was called Gabriel. Gabriel stands in the very presence of God. (See Luke 1:5-25.)

The birth of Jesus is announced to Mary also by the angel Gabriel. He has been sent on a very special assignment to God's chosen woman. There is no indication that Mary was prepared for this sudden visitor from Heaven, so when Gabriel greeted Mary she thought it was a strange greeting. Although she had set her life to serve God, now she was experiencing the favor of God. Mary may not have realized at this point that she was having a visit from an angel. She asked questions to gain more insight into the plans of God.

Even though the angel brought the word of God, it was only through the overshadowing work of the Holy Spirit that Jesus could be conceived. We continue to see how God's plan unfolds when Elizabeth experiences the fullness of the Spirit when Mary visits her (Luke 1:41). The angels were fulfilling their role as messengers from Heaven. It is also significant that both John and Jesus were given their names by an angel (Luke 1:13; 2:21). Adam had been given the authority by God to name every creature. But now the angels named the chosen, signaling a different spiritual authority coming into operation.

During Jesus' early years of life angels continue to communicate the plans and purposes of God. God chose a group of people with the same shepherd's heart as Himself to reveal the birth of Jesus. The angel that appeared to the shepherds no longer came to a temple, a place designated for the glory of God. The angel came and the glory came to those in the hills. It is not surprising that the shepherds were terrified. The heavens continued to open up.

> *Suddenly a great company of the heavenly host appeared with the angel, praising God and saying, "Glory to God in the highest, and on earth peace to men on whom his favor rests"* (Luke 2:13-14).

Even before Jesus went to the cross the heavens were opening. The door that was shut and guarded by the cherubim was opening and the realms of glory were becoming visible. This must have been the most extraordinary worship time for the shepherds. The shepherds' lives must have turned upside down as they found everything exactly as the angels had told them.

Joseph experienced angelic visitations in dreams. Angels told him about the conception of Jesus through the Holy Spirit, which must have been a relief to him! He knew the child was not his but whose was He? Joseph obeyed the angel and took Mary as his wife (Matt. 1:24). His family also escaped death and fled to Egypt because of an angel in a dream and they returned safely back to Israel following another angelic dream.

The scene has now been set for a fresh day and release of the economy of the Kingdom of God.

When Jesus is 30 years old He enters the final and key phase of His ministry on earth. His mother is well aware of the promises of God she had stored in her heart and Jesus knows that He has to be baptized to fulfill all righteousness. He goes to His cousin John the Baptist who has been sent to prepare the way. John states that One is coming after him who will baptize people in the Holy Spirit and with fire. Despite John's reluctance he agrees to baptize Jesus.

> *When all the people were being baptized, Jesus was baptized too. And as He was praying, heaven was opened and the Holy Spirit descended on Him in bodily form like a dove. And a voice came from heaven: "You are my Son, whom I love; with You I am well pleased." Now Jesus Himself was about thirty years old when He began His ministry. He was the son, so it was thought, of Joseph* (Luke 3:21-23).

The words that God spoke and the timing are very significant. The Holy Spirit who came on Jesus is also called the Spirit of Sonship. Jesus was thought to be the son of Joseph. Now God is declaring that Jesus belongs to Him. God is saying more than Jesus is His Son, He was declaring that Jesus is His very representative. This means that the word of Jesus is the same as the word of the Father. The Father is so confident in His son that He will affirm His every word and action. We know that Jesus said He would only do what He saw his Father doing and only say what He heard the Father say. Jesus is the perfect representative.

After His baptism the Holy Spirit immediately leads Jesus into the first challenge to overcome the devil. Jesus came from Heaven announced by the angels and was born by a virgin into mankind. His arrival resulted in an open Heaven as He provided the way for the Holy Spirit to come and permanently live in Him. Now, for Jesus to fulfill His call and commission from the Father, He has to open the way back from earth into the presence of the Father. To provide the way back to the Father He had to break the hold of satan on earth. The Holy Spirit led Him on this journey into the wilderness to face the devil. He made Himself a little lower than the angels to reverse the results of the Fall, to reopen the realms of glory.

Jesus did not eat for 40 days. The devil started tempting Jesus. The roots of all the temptations are the same as the ones that Adam and Eve faced in the garden all those years before.

> *When the woman saw that the fruit of the tree was good for food and pleasing to the eye, and also desirable for gaining wisdom, she took some and ate it* (Genesis 3:6).

The devil tried to get Jesus to turn stones into food, which was counteracted by the deep understanding that true food only comes from the Father. Then the devil showed Him something that looked amazing to the eye—all the kingdoms of the world and their splendor (Luke 4:5-8). The devil tried to get Jesus to worship him. Jesus looked to His Father each time; He was not tempted like Adam and Eve to disobey. Jesus knew all would eventually be His anyway.

The final temptation involved the angelic realm.

> *The devil led Him to Jerusalem and had Him stand on the highest point of the temple. "If You are the Son of God," he said, "throw Yourself down from here. For it is written: "'He will command His angels concerning you to guard you carefully; they will lift you up in their hands, so that you will not strike your foot against a stone.'" Jesus answered, "It says: 'Do not put the Lord your God to the test'"* (Luke 4:9-12).

The Scripture is true; God was able to command His angels. But at this point the angels had not been released to serve those who would inherit salvation. If Jesus had fallen to this temptation it would have been as if He was pulling the angels down to earth with Him, bringing them to a place where they, too, would have had to submit to the work of the devil. Jesus resisted this temptation.

When Jesus was on the cross He faced the same temptation to call on the angels to rescue Him. Even then if He had done so, the plans and purposes of God could never have been fulfilled.

At the end of the temptation: Jesus said to him, *"Away from Me Satan! For it is written: 'Worship the Lord and serve Him only.'" Then the devil left Him, and the angels came and attended Him* (Matt. 4:10-11).

The victory that Jesus won here is highly significant; He caused the reversal of the authority structure on earth. This is why in Romans it refers to Jesus as the second Adam. Adam and Eve should have resisted the serpent in this way in the Garden of Eden, and then the realms of the glory presence of God would never have been closed. Our eyes would never have been closed to the angelic realms. The world would have been very different.

At this point the victory that Jesus brought is only for Him to experience. He begins a journey to bring the victory for anyone who will receive it. Part of the change that happens here includes the angels coming to attend to Jesus.

As we have seen, angels are sent to serve those who inherit salvation—Jesus is the first. Angels are no longer restricted to only bringing messages from the throne room. Now they have been released to come and serve Jesus. The things that happen from this point on in the life of Jesus are fully assisted by the angelic realm. We have the model now open for every believer.

Teachings of Jesus

Jesus speaks about the angels on a number of occasions.

1. Acknowledgement before angels.

   There is clearly quite a bit of talking that goes on in Heaven. As we acknowledge Jesus we can actually gain a reputation in Heaven. We know that Paul was known by the demons. It's even more amazing to be known by the angels.

   I tell you, whoever acknowledges Me before men, the Son of Man will also acknowledge him before the angels of God. But he who disowns Me before men will be disowned before the angels of God (Luke 12:8-9).

   When we step out and share our faith we cause things to happen around us in the heavenly realms. I actually believe that there are angels waiting to spring into action when believers spring into action.

2. Celebration of salvation.

I also believe that Heaven is always enjoying times of celebration. There is great rejoicing over everyone who turns to God.

In the same way, I tell you, there is rejoicing in the presence of the angels of God over one sinner who repents (Luke 15:10).

3. Angels don't know everything.

We might think that because angels are in the very presence of God that they would know everything. This is not the case; there are things that God has chosen not to reveal to the angels. When the prophets were prophesying about the coming of Christ, they knew that there were many details that they did not know about the salvation that was coming. We are told, *"Even angels long to look into these things"* (1 Peter 1:12). This means that there are many plans of God that satan has no idea about.

The timing of the return of Christ is something that the Father has told no one. This is the ultimate secret, the date known only by the Father. Our responsibility on earth is to ensure that as many people as possible have opportunity to join the celebration party.

No one knows about that day or hour, not even the angels in heaven, nor the Son, but only the Father (Matthew 24:36).

4. The end of the age.

Jesus speaks a number of times about the end of the age. One thing that is clear is when Jesus returns in power and great glory the angels will be involved. We are told that angels will come and gather the elect:

…They will see the Son of Man coming on the clouds of the sky, with power and great glory. And He will send His angels with a loud trumpet call, and they will gather His elect from the four winds, from one end of the heavens to the other (Matthew 24:30-31; see also Matthew 25:31).

5. Into the presence of God.

The time came when the beggar died and the angels carried him to Abraham's side (Luke 16:22).

I love the thought that when the day comes to go home the victory is not to an angel of death but to our heavenly Father who sends His angel of life to carry us into His very presence.

6. Eternal fire prepared for satan and his angels.

Then He will say to those on His left, 'Depart from Me, you who are cursed, into the eternal fire prepared for the devil and his angels. For I was hungry and you gave Me nothing to eat, I was thirsty and you gave Me nothing to drink, I was a stranger and you did not invite Me in, I needed clothes and you did not clothe Me, I was sick and in prison and you did not look after Me' (Matthew 25:41-43).

This passage is a significant one in our walk with God. We see time and time again that our actions are important before God. The challenge for us is to *live* the life, not just talk about it. We see in this passage that eternal fire was not made as a place for people to go. It was made as a place for satan and his evil angels to be destroyed. We have a place prepared for us to live in—Heaven (see John 14)—but if we do not make our residence there and demonstrate our faith by how we live then there is only one other place to go for eternity. That is the place prepared for satan.

The End of Jesus' Life

During the life of Jesus there is very little mention of the work of the angels, although they are clearly working with Him to bring the purposes of Heaven on earth. At the end of His life on earth we see again a fresh level of angelic activity. They have a role in helping the disciples embrace Jesus after His resurrection.

In the garden of Gethsemane Jesus took some time to pray. This was the time when He was facing the cross and the full weight of what was to come. While He was praying He even sweated drops of blood, in the process reversing the curse of creation. During this time of prayer Jesus was using every last bit of energy and an angel came to Him from Heaven and strengthened Him for the time ahead (Luke 22:43).

After His death an angel came from Heaven; his appearance was visible and dramatic. There was a violent earthquake and the angel came and moved the stone away from the tomb before sitting on it (Matt. 28:2). This shows us the supernatural strength of angels as the natural obstacle is easily moved. The guards who saw the angel are so shocked by the bright appearance and white clothes that they shook violently and were in such a state that it seemed as if they were dead.

When the women arrived they were greeted with the now familiar greeting, "Do not be afraid" and then the angel spoke of Jesus' resurrection and that they should go and tell the other disciples. Mary also saw two angels in the tomb of Jesus sitting where His body had been (Luke 24:4).

Later when two of the disciples are walking on the road to Emmaus (John 20) they are discussing everything that had happened. They refer to a vision that the women have had. I find this fascinating; the ladies had not referred to a vision, although others described it that way.

The angels continue their involvement right up to the resurrection of Jesus. As He is taken up to Heaven two angels appear. They have come to redirect the attention of the disciples. I think that I would have been like them—standing there staring up into the sky. After all, it's not every day that you see something like that happen. The angels simply tell them that Jesus is coming back in the same way that He has gone.

Now the scene has been set for the days of the greatest angelic activity on earth. Heaven has been waiting for the day when the sons of God can work together with the Holy Spirit and the angels from Heaven.

Chapter 10

The Church and the Angels

The Church is born on the day of Pentecost. Those who had obeyed and waited experienced the outpouring of the glory of God. We have previously looked at the parallels between Ezekiel and Acts. With the change in authority that came through the resurrection of Jesus the angels are now in full operation. They are released to work with people; they are part of the partnership of Heaven and earth. The expectation of the early Church is best seen after Peter has been imprisoned.

Everyday Occasions

The Book of Acts demonstrates that angelic visitations were common in the life of the early Church. It is easy to forget as we read the Scriptures that the pressure on the early believers was at an extremely high level. They were suffering persecution at the hands of King Herod and they had to totally depend on God to stay in a place of peace. It was a time of pain and suffering. Herod killed James, the brother of John. This was not the first time a believer was martyred for their faith. Before the Church had time to regroup, Herod, having seen the pleasure the Jews took in the death of James, had Peter arrested (Acts 12).

Herod held Peter in prison until the Passover observance was over. It was this delay in sentencing Peter that gave the Church an opportunity to gather together to pray—and see a shift in the heavenly realm. The Church prayed without ceasing, knowing this was another life and death situation. Herod was determined not to let Peter escape. The stories of previous escapes made this a particularly sensitive issue, so two guards were assigned to Peter and chained with him in the prison. Just to make sure nothing would go wrong, the door was also being guarded by other soldiers.

The scene was set for a fresh intervention of God. When we understand that we have the full force of Heaven backing us then even in these impossible situations we know God can break through. We saw this in the life of Jesus when He said He knew He could call the full force of Heaven to help but did not do so, as it would have hindered the plan of God from being fulfilled.

Because of Peter's strong faith he was able to sleep even in this situation. While he was sleeping, God sent an angel to bring about the heavenly adventure. When Heaven invades, things often happen suddenly. The plans of Heaven may have been in place for some time but the execution of them on earth results in sudden changes. When the angel appeared, a light shone in the prison cell. The angel was not being gentle as he hit Peter in the side and woke him from his sleep. Instantly, the chains that were holding him fell off. The angel took charge and told Peter to get dressed. Peter thought he was seeing a vision as he was led past the guards (it is not clear if they were asleep or just did not see them). Even the doors swung open by themselves to allow Peter and the angel to pass through.

After they were safely outside, the angel, who had finished his supernatural work, left Peter as suddenly as he had arrived. The angel only needed to be involved when there was a need for the supernatural. The angel did the bit that Peter could not do. When he had escaped it was up to Peter to take some action. This is a very important aspect to understand about God's partnership with us through the angelic. It was only at this point that Peter realized that he was delivered by an angel of God. Perhaps God made Peter think he was having a dream or vision so that his flesh did not stop him from walking through the danger zone to freedom.

Peter considered this miraculous escape from prison and went straight to the house of his friends. They were still there in the middle of the night praying that Peter would be released. They understood that there was a time to pray and a time to sleep. Now was the time to pray. What happened next might seem extraordinary to us.

> *Peter knocked at the outer entrance, and a servant girl named Rhoda came to answer the door. When she recognized Peter's voice, she was so overjoyed she ran back without opening it and exclaimed, "Peter is at the door!"*
>
> *"You're out of your mind," they told her. When she kept insisting that it was so, they said, "It must be his angel."*
>
> *But Peter kept on knocking, and when they opened the door and saw him, they were astonished. Peter motioned with his hand for them to be quiet and described how the Lord had brought him out of prison* (Acts 12:13-17).

Rhoda's response is like an excited child. It makes me think of times when I have called at a friend's house and their children looked through the glass door and rushed off excited, leaving me at the door. Rhoda is so excited that she runs inside with the news that Peter is at the door. I guess the fact Peter did not follow her into the house did not help her argument. At the moment of joy she is told that she is out of her mind. At least she was rewarded by having her name written in the Bible.

Even though the people had been praying well into the night they didn't have the capacity to believe that God was going to respond to their prayers. As Rhoda holds her nerve and is consistent with her story they finally come to the conclusion that I doubt any of us would come up with today–they tell her it's probably Peter's angel. Even though they were praying for Peter to be released they found it easier to believe it was his angel rather than Peter at the door.

I have often wondered how we would react today in a similar situation. First, I doubt that we would think an angel was at the door. If we didn't think it could be Peter we would conclude that it was someone who sounded and looked like him. It is interesting to see that they thought it was *Peter's* angel.

My wife was traveling back home with a team of people after a mission abroad. She woke up in the middle of the night and asked Tony, one of the other members of the team, what he was doing out of his seat. Another member of the team pointed out that Tony was actually asleep in his chair. When Sue described the angel, he looked just like Tony. He was dressed in the same style of clothes, although slightly different from what he was wearing that night. Maybe she saw his angel!

I think that today half of the Church would run to the door for the chance to see something supernatural. The other half would remain seated in unbelief or hide in fear of an invasion from Heaven. The reaction of the early Church in Acts is not one we would see today. Their heads were not turned at the thought of an angel. Eventually Peter's friends went and opened the door; it says that they were astonished that he was standing there.

The reaction of the early believers indicates to me that the appearance of angels and other supernatural phenomena were a normal part of church life. They had seen many miracles and countless salvations over the previous months. The appearance of an angel was not something to distract them; they understood that they were always around and often made appearances while doing their work.

The Church today has lost much of this living expectation of the supernatural. Some of the signs and wonders that had taken place are not common in the current Western church. We are often happy with some manifestation of the gifts of the Spirit and are looking for an increase in healings. The realm of deliverance has some acceptance but takes place in back rooms, avoiding the chance of upsetting anyone. Maybe we don't want to risk being seen as extreme.

It is time for the angelic realm and the heavenly realms to become part of our everyday language and expectations. Earlier in the book we looked at the Garden of Eden from the eyes of Adam and Eve before the Fall. I am personally looking forward to seeing this ability restored to the Church. Every time I read the Bible I get excited about these experiences becoming normal in my life time. I want to get to the place where visible angelic encounters are commonplace.

There are a number of other accounts of angelic action in the book of Acts, each one gives us further understanding.

Escape from Prison
(Acts 5)

The previous story was not the only time Peter had been released from prison by angels. Another time he was imprisoned with all the apostles. Great crowds had been forming because of the many miracles that had taken place. The jealousy of the high priests, who loved attention, resulted in the apostles being imprisoned overnight. But the Lord was not having any of this. He sent one of His angels to open the door and tell the apostles to get out in the morning and continue to preach the Gospel. This is exactly what happened. The faith of the disciples must have grown dramatically as they saw how God was looking after them. This story demonstrates to me how we need to expect angelic action around us. The Holy Spirit has the job to work in and through us, the angelic can bring a whole fresh dimension to life. They are God's agents of action!

Philip and the Ethiopian Eunuch
(Acts 8)

This story interests me as we have both the Holy Spirit *and* angels bringing direction.

> *Now an angel of the Lord said to Philip, "Go south to the road—the desert road—that goes down from Jerusalem to Gaza." So he started out, and on his way he met an Ethiopian eunuch, an important official in charge of all the treasury of Candace, queen of the Ethiopians* (Acts 8:26-27).

Philip would not have even left home if he had not listened to the instructions of the angel. He did listen and sets out on his way. This fresh stage of his life had been initiated by an angelic encounter. As he followed this instruction it is the Holy Spirit within him who instructs him to go closer to the chariot of the eunuch. We see the eunuch coming to faith and being baptized, then Philip is transported elsewhere by the Spirit.

An Angel Visits Cornelius
(Acts 10)

Cornelius was not a believer, yet he attracted the attention of Heaven through his prayers and his generosity to the poor. His action had been remembered in Heaven and resulted in an angel being sent to him in a vision. In the chapter on hospitality we also look at attracting the attention of Heaven and angels. The way we live has a major effect on what supernatural things happen around us. God wants us to provoke Heaven through every means. Cornelius did not just pray, he was generous. We need to do everything we can on earth, knowing that it will cause things to happen in the heavenly realm. The effect of Cornelius' actions made him and his family the focal point for the first Pentecost experience for the Gentiles; the opening of the revelation that the Gospel was not just for the Jews.

The experience of Cornelius makes me wonder what we will see God do in response to *our* faithfulness!

Paul and the Angel

Paul was under arrest with some other prisoners and was being transported by ship to Italy. Things were not looking good and Paul warned them if they continued there would be great loss of life. Despite his advice they decided to continue and sailed straight into a major storm. The men did not eat for a very long time. In the middle of the storm an angel came and stood with Paul. This must have been an amazing time for Paul, for he was standing alone praying that God would break through. Part of the message from the angel was not the most uplifting in the world but it did give Paul an understanding of the direction that God was taking him. It was like hearing that everyone else would be alright but you have a bit more trouble ahead.

> Last night an angel of the God whose I am and whom I serve stood beside me and said, 'Do not be afraid, Paul. You must stand trial before

Caesar; and God has graciously given you the lives of all who sail with you' (Acts 27:23-24).

God has so many ways of communicating and making His strength known.

Angels in the Book of Revelation

The Book of Revelation is a book of images and pictures that often hide the purposes of God. The understanding of the book only comes by the Holy Spirit. The book is a revelation of Christ revealed to John by His angel.

> *The revelation of Jesus Christ, which God gave Him to show His servants what must soon take place. He made it known by sending His angel to His servant John, who testifies to everything he saw—that is, the word of God and the testimony of Jesus Christ* (Revelation 1:1-2).

The indications in the Book of Revelation are that each church has an angel assigned to it.

> *The mystery of the seven stars that you saw in My right hand and of the seven golden lampstands is this: The seven stars are the angels of the seven churches, and the seven lampstands are the seven churches* (Revelation 1:20).

In the passage that follows, the Word of God for each church is written to the angel. The angel is given the responsibility to carry the word and make it available to the church. There is something about the word being written in Heaven that makes it permanent and not a passing word. As believers in the Church the word is also available to us through the Holy Spirit.

Worship in Heaven

The shepherds who were in the fields during the time of Jesus' birth witnessed a life-changing glimpse of the worship in Heaven. In Revelation this experience is expanded even further.

> *Then I looked and heard the voice of many angels, numbering thousands upon thousands, and ten thousand times ten thousand. They*

encircled the throne and the living creatures and the elders. In a loud voice they sang:

"Worthy is the Lamb, who was slain, to receive power and wealth and wisdom and strength and honor and glory and praise!" Then I heard every creature in heaven and on earth and under the earth and on the sea, and all that is in them, singing:

"To Him who sits on the throne and to the Lamb be praise and honor and glory and power, for ever and ever!" The four living creatures said, "Amen," and the elders fell down and worshiped (Revelation 5:11-14).

This must have been an amazing sight, so many angels that it was impossible to count them all. The living creatures we looked at previously were around the throne of glory. They sang in one voice about the worthy lamb, giving Him praise and honor. In Revelation 7 there is even more depth of this awesome worship.

If you continue to look through the Book of Revelation it is clear that the angels are fully involved in everything that is going on.

Chapter 11

GUESTS FOR DINNER

One intriguing passage in the New Testament that mentions angels does so in the same context as entertaining strangers.

Keep on loving each other as brothers. Do not forget to entertain
strangers, for by so doing some people have entertained angels without
knowing it (Hebrews 13:1-2).

Have you thought that you might have entertained angels and not
known? I would be delighted to entertain angels but I would love to
know that I have. This is a very important passage for the Church.
So often we think that hospitality is entertaining our friends. True
hospitality is entertaining those we do not know. It is a vital part of
our Christian life that we are open to people.

Angels can look just like humans. They can walk into your house,
eat your food, and drink your drink. There is nothing that distin-
guishes a genuine stranger from an angel. Maybe after they leave
you wonder, "Was that an angel?" While I have been preparing this
book I have heard many stories about angels. The following couple

of stories left someone wondering if they had just had an encounter with an angel.

David Powell, who lives in England, relayed a story that occurred on December 23, 1987. His grandmother had not been well so he went to spend the day with her. While he was in the south of the country he decided to go to London to a meeting where Jean Darnell was ministering. The meeting finished at 11 P.M. and Dave went straight back to his home in Manchester. He set off in his car and followed the main roads north.

As time went on, the monotony of driving combined with the late night, made him sleepy. The farther he traveled, the more erratic his driving became due to extreme tiredness. Even though it was the middle of winter, the weather was reasonably good and the roads were clear of traffic. There was no lighting in the area, so other than the headlights of his car there was darkness all around. Suddenly he was aware of going past a shadow at the side of the road. He braked hard and stopped.

He saw a man by the side of the road, so he wound down the window and spoke to the man who claimed that his car had broken down. He asked for a lift to the next phone box or service station. This seemed a bit strange as there had been no evidence of any car but Dave felt safe enough to fulfill the man's request. They started to drive along and initially the man thought that a service station would be the best option. Dave said that he was taking the highway all the way to Manchester. Dave felt at ease with his passenger and when he asked if he could have a lift to Stoke, 120 miles away, he was happy to oblige.

As they were going along the man said that he was in the army and was heading home to Stoke. Then he asked a few questions about where Dave had been that evening. It was getting very late when they reached Stoke, conversation had long since stopped. The company had helped Dave stay alert. He found a bright place to stop; the man thanked him and got out of the car. Dave pulled away and looked back in the direction of the man. He was no more than five yards from the drop off point, yet the man had disappeared.

Had he entertained a stranger unawares? As you might imagine, the rest of the journey was no problem as Dave was wide awake wondering. It is possible that this intervention from Heaven kept Dave safe as he went home.

The following amusing story is one that makes us think. It is written by Pastor Chris Girvan from a village near Wrexham in Wales. I have also included a couple of his thoughts after the event.

The year was around 1995. I was a pastor in Port Glasgow, a ship-building town. I had one of those situations in life that just makes you wonder, "Did I or didn't I just entertain an angel"? I don't know if you know what I mean; on one level it is what it is, but on another, you think there is more to it, if we could just probe beneath the event.

Well, my event happened on a winter's night. I remember the winter because the snow was lying thick on the ground. When the weather forecaster says there will be snow on the hills of Scotland, you listen! Our home was on one of those hills—on the top of the hill overlooking the Clyde.

It was 1:30 in the morning when I heard a knock at the door. I pulled on a robe and went downstairs. The estate in which we lived could be very rough and tough so I was a bit nervous. I thought of waking my wife and getting her to answer the door but I thought better of it. I was more scared of my wife being wakened out of her sleep than anything the wilds of Scotland could have at the door.

I opened the door to discover an elderly lady dressed in what I would describe as 1960 fashion wear, black hat, matching black gloves and handbag, very tasteful, 1960 style clothing. The lady announced she had come to see her mother.

What to do? Do you say, "Your mum's not in," or, do you say "Come in out of the cold," and find out what's going on. The worldly—I can't be bothered and I want my bed—really wanted to kick in, but there was an old lady on my doorstep. It was a cold night and how could I call myself a Christian if I turned her away?

I invited the lady in, and as she entered I was aware that she was tall, about a head taller than me which would put her around six feet, two or three inches. My wife, upon hearing me invite a woman into the house in the early hours of the morning, came to see what was going on. She looked at the lady and then looked at me as if to say, "What have you got us into now?" I responded with one of those looks that said, "It's not my fault and what was I supposed to do?"

We invited the lady to sit down and asked her where she lived and where she was from and why she was wandering the streets at night. She was not very responsive to any of our questions. We gave her a cup of warm tea to warm and my wife asked if she could look in her bag. There was passport from the 1960s, letters and addresses of housing that had been demolished many years before. There was not one useful means of identification on the lady.

In the end we decided to phone the police. The lady was still not that talkative and looked very comfortable in our armchair in the front room sipping tea. When the police arrived and came into the front room they took in the scene immediately: elderly woman sipping tea, cold night, she needs a lift home. Why waste police time? Just call a taxi. I said, "I don't know this lady I brought her in when she called at our house an hour ago."

The police decided to investigate a little deeper, "Hello dear, who are you?"

"I have just come to see my mummy," she responded.

I gave the police officer a look as I knew they had been suspicious. The lady stood to go with the officers and I became aware that they were all the same size and they seemed to look the same with their red hair and height. Off they went and they shut the door behind them. The next day my wife asked, "Shall we phone the police and find out how things worked out?" I said, "Let's not, let's just put this one down to God, maybe we entertained angels last night and were unaware of it."

To me it is always one of those situations in life that just makes me wonder, "Did I or didn't I?" All I know is that the lady came knocking on our door and needed our help; she needed somewhere to get out of the cold and we were willing to help. If she was not an angel in disguise with her own police escort, a very useful thing to have if you are an angel traveling in disguise, then I know the angels guided her to our door. It is amazing to think that a day will come when Jesus will say, "I was cold and had no where to go but you took me in." And we will say, "When did we take you in?"

I have asked myself why entertaining strangers attracts angelic activity in this way. I believe one answer is that the heart of God is moved by those who are strangers in another country. In Deuteronomy it says: "*And you are to love those who are aliens, for you yourselves were aliens in Egypt*" (Deut. 10:19). In Psalm 146:9 it says: "*The Lord watches over the alien.*"

God expects the believer to understand the plight of the stranger and the person who is a foreigner in the land. We see that in the Old Testament the Israelites were told to remember the time that they lived as foreigners in Egypt. In the New Testament the believer is told to live as a foreigner in this world and not to take part in its ways. To embrace the stranger is to have an understanding of our place on earth. In fact, one of the criteria for widows to receive their allowance is to entertain strangers. (See 1 Tim. 5:10.) I think that the heart of God is looking out for those who are isolated and are strangers. When we are willing to embrace those we do not know and treat them as friends, we are creating a pathway for the angelic to work around us. We do not know what deposits of the Kingdom are left with us with any angelic encounter.

Chapter 12

DEALING WITH THE
DEMONIC

As I have made clear throughout the book we need to be aware of not just the angels but also of the schemes of satan. In Corinthians we are warned: *...in order that Satan might not outwit us. For we are not unaware of his schemes* (2 Cor. 2:11).

As believers we do not need to be afraid in any way of satan, his demons, or his schemes. They are fallen angels; the angels of God have more power than they do. This is true or they would never have been thrown out of Heaven. We have been given more authority than the angels.

It is important as believers that we know our authority in this realm and know how to exercise it, and how to walk away clean. This chapter is not designed to be a comprehensive manual on how to clear out the demonic but is designed to deal with a few of the myths, and give guidance so that believers can walk free and be healed. Every time the demonic is dealt with, a fresh doorway is opened for angelic activity.

I would like to share a story of deliverance that seems similar to Mary Magdalene, who had seven demons cast out of her by Jesus. The life of Mary was so dramatically changed that she was one of those found following Jesus (Luke 8:1-2) and also when Jesus was resurrected He appeared to her (Mark 16:9). When someone is freed of the demonic we can to expect their lives to be forever changed.

My wife Sue was leading a mission team to India to partner with a local ministry—Harvest India. On one occasion the team went into a Hindu village called Inovolu to conduct a medical camp. The medical camp allowed the ministry to share the Gospel with the local village people. After sharing at the medical camp there was an opportunity to preach the gospel. The team had been praying that there would be signs revealing Jesus. The local people crowded in, desperate to receive a blessing. One of the prayers that Sue often prays in these situations is that the Holy Spirit will overshadow each person and form Jesus in them. This prayer is based on the passage of Scripture when the Holy Spirit overshadows Mary when we are told that the Spirit overshadowed her and Jesus was conceived. (See Luke 1:35.)

Sue continued praying this blessing, using every opportunity to hug and embrace the local people. Suddenly when she was praying, one of the ladies she was holding in her arms bent over like a banana. She realized that this was a demonic manifestation. After she calmed the commotion that started among the local pastors, she commanded the demon to leave in the Name of Jesus. As the demons left she commanded them to go to hell and not harm anyone again. It was clear that the lady was being tormented by more than one demon. Sue spoke very quietly, "I sweep the house clean in the name of Jesus." The demons had to obey and started to leave one at a time.

As the ministry continued Sue felt that it would be good for another member of the team Tony to come and join the praying. Tony came over to see what was happening. As he did he said, "It will have to speak in my language if I am going to get involved!" Immediately the Hindu lady changed language and in clear English said, "No, I won't." You can imagine that they were shocked at her response. Four

demons released their hold. There were a number of unusual mani-
festations during this time as the lady spoke in a man's voice, swore
like a trooper, and her eyes were constantly rolling. It was a good
thing that most of the words were not translated as they were told af-
terward that one of the demons had been threatening murder.

At another point during the proceedings the lady tried to run
away, then she appeared to be settled, although Sue was not convinced that things were finished. They gave the lady a drink of
water, immediately she went wild and started manifesting again.
One of the ladies on the team could see the effects of the demonic in
the spirit. It appeared that there was smoke coming out of the
woman's ears. Sue put her fingers in the woman's ears and kept saying, "I sweep the house clean," and told the demon that it could not
stay any longer.

Later it turned out that the demon had told everyone that it took
up residence in the lady after her uncle had been to worship at the
tombs of the ancestors. When he came home, unknown to him, a
spirit of death had come with him. When he arrived at home the
young lady had washed his feet and the demon took advantage of
the moment and went into the lady's ear. Now it had to leave in the
mighty name of Jesus.

When the seventh and last demon left, the woman relaxed and
came to herself. Through the interpreter, Sue asked her if she would
receive Jesus into her life, she did willingly. As with any story I want
to know the long-term fruit of the ministry.

It turned out that the lady had not slept for years and at night she
would go down to the local cemetery and wander around. The cemetery was located near the village well, so the people regularly went
past it to get water. The woman would go out after them, cursing
them, and throwing stones at them. Immediately after her deliverance, though, she went home and, much to her husband's amaze-
ment, slept all night. A few months later she was still in her right
mind, and her family had been born again as had many in her village.
A church was established as a direct result of the deliverance the lady
experienced.

After that time there was a period where an unusual anointing for deliverance rested on Sue's life. It was a time when we learned a number of lessons. If we embrace these lessons we will be in a good position should we need to deal with demonic activity in the future.

Our Commission and Authority

Often people get frightened about dealing with the demonic. Much of this fear comes from wrong teaching and a wrong understanding of our position in Christ. Casting out demons is not something we need to leave to the specialist ministries. Jesus made it clear to the disciples that casting out demons was something that they should expect to do as part of their ministry.

> *And these signs shall accompany them that believe: in my name shall they cast out demons; they shall speak with new tongues; they shall take up serpents, and if they drink any deadly thing, it shall in no wise hurt them; they shall lay hands on the sick, and they shall recover* (Mark 16:17-18 ASV).

When we feel out of our depth it is vital that we get the necessary support so we can grow and the person who is receiving ministry gets the proper care. There are some people who have more experience and have a level of gifting that brings release quickly.

In Chapter 8 we looked at the authority structure in Heaven. We know we are seated with Christ in heavenly places—our life is hidden in Christ.

> *For you died, and your life is now hidden with Christ in God. When Christ, who is your life, appears, then you also will appear with him in glory* (Colossians 3:3-4).

When we understand that our life is hidden in Christ, we realize that satan can not see us coming, he can only see Christ coming! Elsewhere in scripture we're told: *You believe that there is one God. Good! Even the demons believe that—and shudder* (James 2:19).

When a demon sees Christ coming, it shudders, knowing it is defeated.

We have a dog called Madison. I have never seen a breed of dog that has such an understanding of order and authority of the pack. Much to my wife's annoyance, our dog decided that I was top of its pack (even though Sue does most of the work with the dog!) Madison is quite happy to break the rules when no one is around. One of the rules she likes to break is sleeping on our bed. There have been many times when she hears me start to walk up the stairs and leaps off the bed and hides herself away. On one amusing occasion she only got half way off the far side of the bed when I entered the room. She froze—her back legs and tail still on the bed hoping that if she could not see me she could get away with her caper!

Like our dog, demons understand that we have great authority. They can't hide themselves and they know they have to leave.

Ministering to People

When we are removing demons we need to remember we are ministering to people. Sue recounts one experience when the reaction of the people to the demonized person was very aggressive. They dealt with the person as if they were the demon! Jesus would often deal with things in a very discrete way. There have been many occasions when we have seen people delivered of demons in a crowded room, and even those close by were unaware of what was happening.

I remember meeting a person who had become involved with prostitutes and was plagued by demons. Although he had repented and was getting his life sorted out, he was still tormented. He was ministered to discretely and all the demons left him within five minutes without any of the people in the busy meeting knowing what happened. The man was now free to continue his life.

Using Our Authority

When we are dealing with demons we need to remember our authority; shouting and anger are not the same thing. Over the years I have learned that a silent look or quiet firm word is extremely effective with our children. There is no need to demonstrate authority by throwing around our weight—it may impress some people but not demons. Someone with genuine authority does not need to shout or boast; they just quietly get the job done.

When commanding a demon to leave, keep it simple, trust the Holy Spirit and then, as indicated earlier, pray in the name of Jesus, "I sweep the house clean." If you remember your authority, then remember that any demon has to leave and we can deal with them quickly.

Keep Them Quiet

We are told in the Bible that on one occasion Jesus would not allow the demons to speak. If you let them speak they will most likely tell you lies and they will probably give you an incorrect name. Their aim is always to bring confusion and even get you to a place where you don't cast them out. Remember, you do not need to know anything about them to get them to leave.

> *You belong to your father, the devil, and you want to carry out your father's desire. He was a murderer from the beginning, not holding to the truth, for there is no truth in him. When he lies, he speaks his native language, for he is a liar and the father of lies* (John 8:44).

> *Moreover, demons came out of many people, shouting, "You are the Son of God!" But he rebuked them and would not allow them to speak, because they knew he was the Christ* (Luke 4:41).

What Can Demons Do?

It is important that we train ourselves to follow the leading of the Holy Spirit. He is the one who will give us the ability to discern what is happening. There are many times when two sets of circumstances have totally different roots. Evil spirits can cause all sorts of disruption in people's lives. Here are a few situations with which Jesus dealt.

1. Restoring a man to his right mind.

> *When Jesus got out of the boat, a man with an evil spirit came from the tombs to meet him. This man lived in the tombs, and no one could bind him any more, not even with a chain. For he had often been chained hand and foot, but he tore the chains apart and*

broke the irons on his feet. No one was strong enough to subdue him (Mark 5:2-4).

This story is very similar to Sue's account in India earlier in the chapter. When the evil spirits were cleared out, the man was in his right mind.

2. Restoring a child with convulsions.

So they brought him. When the spirit saw Jesus, it immediately threw the boy into a convulsion. He fell to the ground and rolled around, foaming at the mouth. Jesus asked the boy's father, "How long has he been like this?" "From childhood," he answered. "It has often thrown him into fire or water to kill him. But if you can do anything, take pity on us and help us." "'If you can'?" said Jesus. "Everything is possible for him who believes" (Mark 9:20-23).

3. Restoring hearing and sight.

When Jesus saw that a crowd was running to the scene, he rebuked the evil spirit. "You deaf and mute spirit," he said, "I command you, come out of him and never enter him again." The spirit shrieked, convulsed him violently and came out. The boy looked so much like a corpse that many said, "He's dead." But Jesus took him by the hand and lifted him to his feet, and he stood up (Mark 9:25-27).

4. Restoring health.

On a Sabbath Jesus was teaching in one of the synagogues, and a woman was there who had been crippled by a spirit for eighteen years. She was bent over and could not straighten up at all. When Jesus saw her, he called her forward and said to her, "Woman, you are set free from your infirmity." Then he put his hands on her, and immediately she straightened up and praised God (Luke 13:10-13).

Spirits of Infirmity

Demons can cause long-term sickness, often manifesting in a number of different ways. I will always remember when my friend Duncan Smith said that it is easy to spot a spirit of infirmity if the sickness or pain moves when you minister healing. I simply followed the model that he showed me; if a sickness moves, then I know what

I am dealing with. My faith rises as I know it has to leave and the person will recover.

Over recent years we have seen where the removal of evil spirits has resulted in healing of hearing, sight, and many other infirmities. Demons will make the most of any footholds to tie up people's lives. Often a trauma has caused the foothold and the spirit has made the most of the moment. As these spirits are removed people find emotional freedom that they have not previously known. In a number of cases this freedom has been reflected in the person's ability to breathe deeply and freely.

The following testimony shows us a number of effects of satan's destructive schemes as well as God's overriding power to bring restoration. My wife traveled with a small team to the Philippines. While they were there they spent quite a bit of time on one of the local rubbish dumps, feeding the children, and clothing them. In this environment they were able to offer basic medical care. Many of the injuries they saw would not have been found in the Western world. The children had glass wounds causing infections, there were burns, and other untreated ailments.

One day they visited the dump and went into the hut where the care ministry was going to take place. The heavy wooden shutter was propped open with flimsy bamboo poles. Suddenly one of the team was struck with major stomach pains. Sue realized that this was not a natural problem, but the origin was a spirit of infirmity trying to get hold. Acting as if she could see the spiritual realm she grabbed hold of the evil spirit and pulled it off the team member's stomach with great force, pronouncing its hold broken in the name of Jesus.

Immediately the team member was healed. As Sue's hand flew back, the evil spirit left in the direction toward the shuttered window and knocked the bamboo pole down. The shutter slammed shut with major force. Sadly, a 9-year-old boy called Jonjon was peering in the window to see all the activity in the hut. The shutter smashed the back of his head and smashed his face against the wooden sill. He fell to the floor bleeding and unconscious. Everyone raced around to him. It seemed as if the whole work was going to come to a disastrous halt.

Responding automatically to the need, everyone started to pray and command life to return to the boy. There was blood in his mouth and nose, they could not detect any signs of breathing, and his pulse was getting weaker. It seemed an eternity as the boy lay there lifeless while the team was pleading for the healing power of God. All of a sudden the boy started to move one of his fingers and then his hand. He opened his eyes and came round. Sue picked him up and he sat on her lap looking dazed. Within five minutes he was fully recovered, receiving lollipops and brand new clothes!

Get Yourself Clean

Whenever my son comes home from playing in the local soccer team he is covered from head to toe in mud. He did not go out to play in the mud but it is a consequence of the energy that he puts in when he plays the game. The real battle then begins; he is at an age when he does not believe in showers! He gives me that look that tells me he knows what I am going to say and he is making a list in his head of all the different things he has to do before the inevitable happens.

One of the things we learned the hard way is the importance of cleaning ourselves up after we have dealt with the demonic. In the testimony I shared about the lady in India the team did not immediately deal with the evil spirits that had been cast out. When one of the women saw in the spirit that the demons were following the team away from the village, they quickly dealt with them so they could have no further affect.

Now after we deal with the demonic we routinely pray that God will clean us up and nothing will have an ongoing effect. There have been rare occasions when we have not prayed and have found that our lives were affected in the weeks that followed. The way I see it, when you have been in the mud, get yourself clean. Dirt is not a big problem but it will become one if not dealt with.

Conclusion

There is a lot more to say about this area of the spiritual realm—this has been only a taste. One thing we have consistently seen is God by His grace causing people to be unaware of the demons leaving. It is as if God gives the person an anesthetic until the operation is over. Demons are fallen angels that now have the opposite effect from their original purpose. On the other hand, just think, we have angels working on our behalf bringing to us health, healing, sound thinking, and helping us hear and understand the things of Heaven. Remember, every time we deal with an evil spirit we bring the Kingdom to earth.

> *But if I drive out demons by the Spirit of God, then the kingdom of God has come upon you* (Matthew 12:28).

Chapter 13

CHILDREN AND THE
SUPERNATURAL

I have really been looking forward to writing this chapter. I believe that we all have a responsibility to encourage children in their spiritual walk. This is especially applicable to those who have children or grandchildren, or work directly with them. I would specifically like to dedicate this chapter to my three children, Lucy, Tom, and Abbie. They have constantly provoked me in spiritual things, often their insights have left my wife and I shocked. My eldest daughter was only 4 years old when she began having dreams. She continues to have dreams and has the ability to see into the supernatural. Sometimes she sees clearly for a while and then has periods when she does not have dreams or see anything specifically in the angelic. One of her stories is found later in the chapter.

The challenge to us is to support and train our children without squashing them because we do not understand them or think that they are imagining things. My wife and I have determined that we are going to do everything we can to make supernatural things of God accessible to our children and to the children and young people of the local church. I want the children trained to pray for the sick, see signs and wonders, as well as see the angelic realm. I have found that often it is the children who are able to embrace these things quicker than adults.

My challenge to everyone reading this is to hand on to the next generations everything that we have learned over the years, as if it is normal. It took me a number of years to become comfortable with the fact that today God speaks directly to people and through prophecy. I have taught our children that God speaks and we should expect Him to speak into every aspect of life. The same is true in the realms of the supernatural and the angelic.

It is vital that we open ourselves to learn from children about the things of the Kingdom. There are probably many things that we will not learn unless we have their humble attitude. Jesus tackled this issue with His disciples on a number of occasions. In Matthew 18 Jesus calls a little child over and has him stand among the disciples,

> *And he said: "I tell you the truth, unless you change and become like little children, you will never enter the kingdom of heaven. Therefore, whoever humbles himself like this child is the greatest in the kingdom of heaven.*
> *"And whoever welcomes a little child like this in my name welcomes me. But if anyone causes one of these little ones who believe in me to sin, it would be better for him to have a large millstone hung around his neck and to be drowned in the depths of the sea"* (Matthew 18:3-6).

There is a double challenge in this passage. Are we going to be like children and are we going to be those who welcome the children and encourage them to follow God?

It is only a little bit later when the disciples try and stop the children from coming to Jesus. His response is quick and sharp, *"Let the little children come to me, and do not hinder them, for the kingdom of heaven belongs to such as these"* (Matt. 19:14).

I have included a few stories of angelic visitations to children. The first story is from a little girl whose parents are part of the local church. As you read it take time to look at the impact on the little girl. Her life was changed by her angelic encounters. The account of Lydia was recorded for us by her mother, Abigail Brown:

> Lydia loved her first semester of going to school full time, but after term break she started having tremendous problems. She cried and screamed every time I brought her into school. It was awful and I started to dread taking her in every morning. This behavior was totally out of character for Lydia. She told me she just missed me so much. The weeks following this were very hard, I would drop her off at the school and go home and cry. All was soon to change as God had other ideas.
>
> God told me to give it all over to Him, the worry and the hurt, as He knew Lydia a lot better than I did. He simply said, "Trust me, for I'm your Dad." With these simple words and after a lot of heartache and soul searching, eventually I let go. The next day Lydia still went into school crying and my heart sank. But I had made a decision to trust and that's what I did.
>
> I was glad that we had come to the weekend. As a family we all kicked into routine. It was dad's weekend to work so off he went, the children were fed and watered, and after a quick run around with the vacuum cleaner, we all went off to the supermarket for a few bits and pieces.
>
> I was in the middle of this rush of family life driving to the supermarket when Lydia turned to me and said very casually and without fuss, "Mum, I had angels in my bedroom last night." She said it as though this was an everyday occurrence. I, on the other hand, found it hard to drive and take in what she had just said. I asked her about a dozen questions at once which Lydia took in stride. She explained that she was a little scared at first when the angels came into her room, but she said they prayed that she wouldn't be scared, so she wasn't. There were a lot of angels, some small, others big; she told me they cuddled her. I was so overwhelmed, "God, thank you so much."

That evening when I put Lydia to bed we thanked God for sending the angels. Lydia said she would ask the angels why they had come. The next morning Lydia bounced into our room saying the angels were praying that I would know God more and they were cuddling me, it was so comfortable. She was radiant and buzzing with such excitement. Then she said, "Mummy, Daddy, do you see angels?" We both shook our heads in mute response. With that Lydia stretched out her hands toward us, "In the name of Jesus I pray that mummy and daddy will see angels in their bedroom. Amen."

Lydia continued to bounce on the bed and told us how the angels had made her laugh by tickling her feet and how funny it all had been. I saw through Lydia how much fun the Kingdom of God is. Lydia was completely thrilled; she was having so much fun with the angels she didn't want to sleep. It was wonderful to see her excitement.

When Monday morning came Lydia told me her "Lydia angel" was going to school with her. Lydia described the angel as being big and called him "Lydia angel" because he was her special angel, even though she referred to the angel as a "Him" she still called him "Lydia angel" and said he was big and comfortable. I asked what she meant by "comfortable" and she explained, "When he cuddles me his feathers are soft and it feels so comfortable."

We got to school and she waved good-bye to me. She had no tears; it was a real miracle and I went home and praised God for all that He had done. For the next couple of weeks "Lydia angel" went to school and from all accounts had a wonderful time. Lydia now sees "Lydia angel" at school on occasions.

It is easy to get very serious about our walk with God and lose the sense of enjoyment and fun. We are told that Jesus had a joy that distinguished him from his peers. Lydia had great fun playing with the angels. For some of us this might be a difficult concept to grasp. The truth is God invented play; it is one of the most important ways that children learn. We need to be like children. I find it amazing that

Lydia spoke of the feathers on the angel and the fact they were so soft. We are told in Psalm 91 that God covers us with his feathers. I believe that this experience with God will stay with Lydia for the rest of her life and be one of those defining moments with God.

As I have indicated, children often find it easier to embrace the heavenly and angelic realms. I have often felt that while I am still trying to find the starting line, the children find it very easy to see. My daughter Lucy has been having dreams most of her life and has an ability to see and understand what is happening in the spiritual realms around her. When she was only 4 years old she had a dream about the specific red car that we were going to buy. When I went down to the local car auction, I was not looking for *any* car but for the red one that was in the dream. We had very limited finances and knowing the popularity of red cars this was going to be an interesting challenge.

As I looked around it was not long before I saw the car; it was the only red car in the auction. All I had to do was to wait and see if it would be in the right price range. When it was time for the car to go through the auction, they could not get it to start by any of their normal means. This was not a good sign and all the other potential bidders quickly dispersed. I waited, confident that this was the car in Lucy's dream. In the end I made the auctioneers push the car through the auction. The bidding was as you might expect, low, and I had quickly sealed the deal. We later managed to get the car started and it was soon on the way home. We only had limited money and God had ensured that this was enough for the complete purchase. We have come to expect these interventions from the children.

On more than one occasion my son Tom and I have stood in my daughter's room and prayed we would have dreams and see angels as she does!

One night when Lucy was 12 years old she came back downstairs having just gone up to bed. She asked if I would go with her and watch her as she climbed up the ladder into her bed. She had one of those elevated beds with a chair and a desk underneath. I was tired and not very keen on following her up the stairs so I asked her why she wanted me to go with her. She explained in a very relaxed manner that there was an angel under her bed and she would have to walk past it to get into bed. It did not bother her that she would be in bed with an angel underneath.

Now I was excited at the opportunity to see this angel. I followed her up to her room and as I entered the room I had to ask Lucy where the angel was. She pointed to it with a look on her face that said it should be obvious. It was not obvious to me. I later asked Lucy to describe the angel—it was nothing like I expected. She told me the angel was about 6 feet tall. The angel was able to get under the bed if he bent over. He had ginger, shoulder-length hair and a very white face. Lucy thought he was about 26 years old. The rest of his body was not distinguishable because it was covered by slightly off white clothes. In his right hand he held a spear.

That was the last we heard from Lucy that night. The next morning she came downstairs and told us that Harry had been under the bed all night. I immediately asked who Harry was—her angel of course. After I left the night before she had asked the angel his name. He told her it was Harry. Lucy was very keen to find out the meaning of his name. We looked it up in one of those books of children's names. I was staggered to find that it came from the name Harold which means army ruler. Lucy continued to see the angel Harold on and off for a number of weeks. One night Lucy actually prayed with the angel when she went to bed. She came and asked if this counted, as the Bible talks about the power of two or more being in agreement. One other thing Lucy told us about this angel was he enjoyed playing. This reinforced my belief that on many occasions, angels, like people, just enjoy themselves.

Suddenly one night the angel left, he had apparently moved up to the hills close to a nearby town and had set up camp with other angels. This part of the story is told later in Chapter 15, which gives some accounts of the activities in the spiritual realm in the area where I live.

It was not long after the angel left that Lucy appeared in our room late at night and complained about the demonic attacks that she was enduring. These attacks manifested themselves visually to her. They appeared as vicious eagles, bees, angry bulls, and other animals.

Each time she came back to our room we tried to help her use her own authority to deal with the attacks.

Eventually it was clear that she was too tired and each time she dealt with one attack another came. She could not get the final breakthrough. She came in and said, "I just can't take anymore!" I was also getting tired and bravely offered to swap rooms. I felt extra bold as I climbed my way up to her bed—I'm not partial to heights. As I lay down to sleep I was suddenly bombarded by a barrage of demonic-inspired words. This shocked me and I commanded the demon to leave the house before rolling over and going to sleep.

In the previous chapter we will take a brief look at the demonic realm and how to deal with it should it manifest in some way around us. We need to understand that when people develop the ability to see they may see both angelic and demonic activity.

I share this story so that we can think about encouraging our children in everything that God has for them. They are often more aware than we are of the heavenly realms. We can help them explore these realms and at the same time allow ourselves to be challenged by their experiences. It is very easy for adults to minimize children's spiritual experiences and exploration by telling them that the things they are experiencing are only their imagination. If we do this we are not training them to see into the realms of the spirit.

Yes, it is possible that some of the things children say are from their imagination. Each child will have a different level of sensitivity to spiritual things. We can teach our children to operate in their God-given authority to pray and even command things that may try and affect them to leave. As parents, we also believe that we need to take our position and provide spiritual and natural protection for our children. They face many things each day and not all of them are easy to throw off. If we allow demonic things to have a foothold in our house they will take advantage of this.

We learned many years ago the importance of taking full authority in our house. Our children would have nightmares and be disturbed by different things. We started by praying around our house that no demonic things would touch our house. Although things were peaceful in the house, unusual things continued to happen.

During this time my son had a nightmare where he was attacked by something demonic. In his sleep he commanded it to leave and it left rapidly through our bedroom, but woke Tom up in the process. He came into our room. My wife, at the same moment, awoke with the feeling that an animal had bounced on her and gone out through the window. This was another lesson to us about our authority in the spiritual realm.

One of the things that happened during this time was our pet rabbit developed a large growth (we had not prayed that our garden would be covered). The vet told us that there was no cure and the rabbit would die within six months. We bought a replacement for him. My daughter prayed for the rabbit and we saw the growth literally drop off over a period of time and the skin heal over. The older rabbit has outlived the new one we had purchased!

These personal stories help us understand that we live with a spiritual world. There are many activities going on and it is vital that we position ourselves correctly and use the authority that God has given us to live in life. Not everything that comes from the spiritual world is good. We have full authority to deal with anything demonic and as believers do not have to live under it. As you learn, train the children at the same time. You will be amazed what God will do. We have found out so much as a family and discovered the importance of asking God's protection on every area of our lives.

There is one more story about children and the heavenly realms. My wife heard this story while on a missionary trip in the Philippines.

In a very remote village called Mindinoa there was a small group of believers. Most of them did not have the ability to read and write, and the church had gained a local reputation for singing well known choruses with their own local twist. One Sunday morning the church was meeting together worshiping God. They were all very surprised to see a white bird fly into the meeting place. The bird was not one that any of the local people recognized.

It caught their attention, and did not panic as it flew around the room. There was a large banner on the wall of the building, which had the words Holy Spirit printed on it. They were amazed when it fluttered by the words Holy Spirit. The bird finally flew back out of the meeting place. Later in the day a few of the children from the Sunday school went back into the main hall to "play church." After a while some of the adults returned to the church hall to find all of the children lying flat out on the floor caught up by the presence of God. When the children eventually woke up they all told how they had been with Jesus in Heaven and while they were there He showed them where the white bird lived.

May I encourage you to tell some of these stories to your children or youngsters you might have in your care. We have noticed how children get caught up and enjoy hearing stories about other children. Encourage them in the realms of the spirit at any opportunity!

Chapter 14

WHEN ANGELS
APPEAR TODAY

Earlier in the book I recounted how the involvement of an angel was the difference for me between life and death. This story is by no means unique. In the Kingdom of God there are those pioneers who are willing to risk their lives to make a difference in the world. I believe that in this realm there is a release of angelic and supernatural help that would not otherwise be seen. Angels are involved in warning people as well as leading people out of dangerous situations. The following is one such story from my friend Dave Cooke.

Dave is an ordinary guy who has risked everything, and in the process helped millions of children and young people to have a moment of happiness. He was one of the people who did not just watch the plight of the Romanian orphans on television. He took action and motivated others to do the same. He is best known as the founder of Operation Christmas Child which collects and distributes millions of shoeboxes each Christmas to children around the world who would otherwise have nothing.

In October 1993 during the height of the war in Bosnia, Dave was with three other men traveling the very dangerous route from Croatia to Sarajevo for some meetings the next day. They were making preparations for the next shoebox distribution right into the middle of this well-publicized disaster area. The four men had hired an ordinary car with Croat number plates. The weather was typical for the time of the year, with thunder, lightning, and the first light snowfall sticking on the ground. It was not the ideal time to be traveling along the potholed roads, even without the ever-present danger of sniper fire.

As they came to the hills surrounding Sarajevo, darkness had fallen. They stopped at an army command post to refuel. Due to the extreme danger they were advised by the army not to go any further that night. But a number of the team were desperate to get to the meeting the next day so they continued down the road against this advice.

They had not gone much farther when the wheel of the car went into a large hole in the road caused by a scud missile. The tire blew out, but it was fortunate that there was a spare. They quickly changed the wheel and moved on. The situation only got worse; the roads were totally bombed out. It was not long before the car hit another mine hole in the road, damaging the wheel.

The village they were in was deserted and they needed tools to try and straighten out the wheel and refit the tire. They knocked on the door of a nearby house and a Muslim lady answered the door. She had the tools they needed but made it clear to them that it was not safe to continue down the road to Sarajevo. Partly due to the adrenalin rush, the team did not heed these warnings and wanted to press on to their destination. Having mended the wheel they set off again in appalling weather conditions. Suddenly they came around a corner and the headlights shone straight at a car in the middle of the road in front of them. The owner of the car was spread-eagled across the hood with guns pointed at his head. He was about to be executed.

Disturbed by the lights the gunmen let the man go and as he jumped back into his car they smashed all the windows and he sped off into the night. The driver of Dave's car reacted quickly in the situation, drove into a field, spun the car around and returned back to the previous village to find shelter for the night. They found the Muslim lady and she allowed the four men to spend the night in her house. There was no food, running water, or electricity available. Dave could not sleep due to the extreme cold. They were all relieved when the new day dawned and they could continue on their way.

As the men went out through the village they saw the field where they had turned around the previous night. There were clear warning signs to keep out because the field was mined. The hand of God had kept them safe at a time of extreme danger. Later they went back through the village and found some local people. They asked where the lady lived who had been so generous to them. They were told that there was no such person in the village. In fact no one lived in the village. It was a Muslim village that had been cleared out during the ethnic cleansing that had taken place. In the middle of grave danger, God, by His grace, had sent an angel to provide a safe place.

Dave's comment on the events was very significant; he told me that this type of war situation was new to him at the time so the adrenalin was pumping. It was as if he took everything in his stride at the time and did not realize the significance until after the experience. He said, "I think if I had realized I would have been inquisitive, asked questions, and could have upset the boat."

This reminds me of the experience mentioned previously of Peter in the Book of Acts when an angel came and led him out of prison.

> *Then Peter came to himself and said, "Now I know without a doubt that the Lord has sent His angel and rescued me from Herod's clutches and from everything the Jewish people were anticipating." When this had dawned on him...* (Acts 12:11-12).

We have seen how angels are sent to serve the people of God. I wonder, are some of our angels sitting waiting for us to enter into some adventures with God so they can take their place and so we can see unusual supernatural things happen?

Healing in India

My wife Sue has visited India on a number of occasions. During one visit the team was going to a small Hindu village to officially open a church building. While they were praying beforehand the Holy Spirit showed them that this was a place where He wanted to open a healing well. They also felt that the pastor had a significant healing ministry. When they arrived they met the pastor who shared his remarkable testimony.

As a young man the pastor had led a colorful life and consequently had contracted HIV, which progressed to full blown AIDS. Later he became a Christian and went to Bible College. As the sickness took hold, his weight plummeted from 176 pounds to 88 pounds. He spent great sums of money on medication while at the same time asking God for healing. He started to put weight on, but thought this was probably due to the medication. He would go up into the mountain to pray and read the Bible. He had been doing this for about six months when a so-called friend offered him a strange fruit, telling him that it would make him better. He got worse and went off to the hospital. They told him the shocking news that the fruit was poisonous and with it in his system he would not live for more than a day.

The young man discharged himself from the hospital and dragged himself up the mountain for one last time. He prayed, telling God that he could not take the pain any more. Crying and shaking, he apologized to God and prepared himself to leap off the mountain to his death. Suddenly he heard the sound of angels singing around him. He did not know their language but joined in the heavenly chorus. A huge angel appeared in front of him and he felt something like a beam of light transfer into him. He was instantly and totally healed from all his illnesses and received a healing impartation. At this point he realized that God had given him a second chance. He said, "God I am going to give my entire life to you." He went straight off to a Hindu village and started to pioneer a church. As he told his testimony people began to gather looking for healing. This was the church my wife had the privilege of visiting, and she noticed that this area has a significant specialty hospital based near the church. The natural is reflecting God's plans for the region.

Angels are often directly involved in healing. They are God's agents bringing dimensions of Heaven and making them available on earth.

God Is Into Detail

As well as these life-changing moments I believe that God wants to work on our behalf to release heavenly provision, simply to bless us and show us how powerful He is.

Dave Cooke was returning home in 1992 from Romania having helped build a new orphanage. He was thinking about the next day when he was heading off on vacation with his wife. He arrived at Cluj Napoco airport for the short flight to Bucharest before the longer flight home to the United Kingdom. The interpreter had already left and there was no one around who spoke English. Dave was told that he was not booked on the flight and there was no more space.

At a loss about what to do, he started to pray. He felt challenged about prayer. It's ok to pray but do I really believe that God is able to do miracles on my behalf? Having wrestled with this Dave felt peaceful and waited to see what would happen. Suddenly someone came up to him and said "Mr. Cooke, you may fly. There is one seat spare." It seemed as if his problems were over, until he reached Bucharest. Again he was told that there was no room on the flight and he would have to join the queue for standby passengers. He noticed that the Romanian locals were getting on the flight ahead of him. This was happening at a time when the airport in Bucharest did not have computers to issue boarding passes and organize bookings.

When he asked questions Dave was told that he should come back in 20 minutes. More than 30 minutes had passed and Dave was still waiting. The rest of the passengers had long since gone to the plane. Suddenly a lady appeared and said, "Follow me." Without a boarding pass Dave was taken through passport control and then bundled in the back of a vehicle. The van drove him around the back of the plane and stopped at the pilot's entrance. Dave was led up the steps and found himself being offered a seat in the business class section. An airhostess came up to him and said "Mr. Cooke, would you like an aperitif?" As he prepared to take off Dave did not know whether to laugh or cry. He knew that God had supernaturally worked on his behalf and made a way where there was no way.

It is easy to think that God will only act on our behalf in certain situations. This true story is an amazing reminder that God will work on our behalf in all sorts of ways. He just loves to bless us. It was important to God that the vacation took place!

In the next chapter we have a number of stories in which angels have been seen through the eyes of the heart. Here is an amusing story to whet your appetite.

There have been a number of occasions when angels have been involved in meetings and bringing about the purposes of God. One particularly fun time I saw an angel walk in behind Tony Howson, one of our leaders, as he was speaking at the annual church holiday event. I did not take too much notice of the angel other than the fact it stood behind Tony and started to play with his hair. As he continued to preach Tony became aware that he was constantly brushing his hair as if to flatten it. As the meeting went on Tony was becoming increasingly touched by the Holy Spirit. By the end it was a bit like the Book of Acts as he appeared to be totally drunk and would admit himself that his words were not coming out right or making much sense. During this time the presence of God was becoming more and more powerful in the room. It was a very significant time for many of the people present as God moved and set them free. The meeting continued late into the evening.

Chapter 15

THROUGH THE EYES
OF MY HEART

Over the past few years I have had the privilege of being around a number of sharp "seers"–believers who have the gift of seeing into the spiritual realm. They have often confirmed the things happening in the spiritual realm around me. There have been a number of occasions when they have told me what was going on in the angelic realms and have helped me grow in this area. As I have said before, not everyone is a seer, but I believe that everyone can learn to see and there are always the "suddenlies" of God!

I have drawn together a number of stories, some of which are my own, others have been kindly given to me to share with you. Many of these accounts I have been able to confirm with a number of people seeing the same things at the same time. They differ from the stories in the previous chapter because they are all seen with the eye of the heart. I hope you enjoy the stories and that they challenge you to ask God to open your eyes to see more.

143

Angels in India

In an earlier chapter dealing with the demonic, there is an amazing story about a lady set free from seven demons. The following account by Claire Dillamore gives an indication of what else was going on in the realms of Heaven during this same time.

Medical Camp at Inovolu

The medical camp and the evening outreach meeting were held in a place called Inovolu. It seemed as if the whole village had turned out. There were groundsheets at the front on which the children and old people were sitting in two distinct groups. There was a bit of a gap behind them and then rows of chairs where the women were seated. The men were hiding in the dark at the back!

We were sitting at the front facing the people and I saw several demons standing behind the back row of children and in front of the women. I looked three times to make sure! I began to pray as the meeting progressed and suddenly a huge angel flew in and stood under the canopy. The demons skulked off into the darkness when they saw him. I felt that the angel was the angel of the church that would be established in that town, and that he carried a healing anointing. The angel did nothing except stand in one place while the meeting continued.

I'm wondering, as I'm writing this, whether it was entirely a coincidence that a frog the size of a dinner plate jumped out at us during the meeting, or that nasty insects came and landed on us as we gave vaccines to the children!

At the end of the meeting, the medical camp was opened and we prophesied that a well would open in that place. As Sue did this the well opened in the spirit and the angel moved to stand by the well and stir the waters. It was after this that the amazing deliverance took place which we recount in chapter 12.

Angels at the Indian Crusade Meetings

There were three crusade meetings. At the first meeting I only saw one or two angels, shepherding angels, ushering the people into the gathering. They also directed the people forward in response to the appeal for salvation at the end.

On the second night the shepherding angels were there again. During the meeting, I saw a golden line of angels in front of people at the front. They were not facing the people, but facing the space. They were there to declare the ground as holy ground. Two thousand people responded to the appeal that night—too many for the space at the front!

When we arrived for the last night of the crusade, the air was literally thronging with angels swooping and flying over the crusade ground. We saw them as flashes of light and could feel the glory cloud in the air above and on the edge of the platform. A worship angel was standing at the end of the keyboard, joining in with the worship team.

When the demons were commanded to leave, hundreds of them spilled into the chasm as huge angels appeared in the air, beating them with sticks. I had to look twice because I thought that fighting angels ought to have swords. When we talked this through later, we realized that sticks are used to kill snakes. The day before, a poisonous snake had been killed on the grounds of the Bible college.

The Eagle

The supernatural realm can manifest itself in many forms. At one gathering of the church, Dan Slade, a visiting speaker from the Ukraine, was invited to speak. The presence of God was very strong on Dan when he suddenly declared that a prophetic eagle was looking from the corner of the room. I personally could not see what he was pointing to, although a number of the congregation immediately had their eyes open to this supernatural visitation. Dan spoke of the eagle bringing the prophetic dimension. This is a clear mark of the local church I am privileged to be part of.

A couple of days later a young lady in another meeting saw an eagle going to the Philippines with a missions team. This eagle was carrying the tools of redemption; it had bread in one foot and wine in the other. She also saw my wife, who was leading the team, covered in silver. The following week a team was indeed traveling to the

Philippines. This was a new venture and the team was going to see if God was bringing a connection for His purposes.

The first night the hosts, Robert and Sarah, joined the team at the hotel and at the end of the evening they decided to pray. While they were praying and prophesying the heart of God, one of the team suddenly saw the eagle in the spirit hovering in the corner of the room. She commented that it looked very kind. When God reveals things in this way He is usually pointing to His purposes at this time. God's plan was to release a new prophetic dynamic to the ministry.

During one of the meetings, the spiritual environment seemed to be squeezing the life out of the gathering. The Holy Spirit made it clear it was time to press back the principalities so the prophetic had room to be expressed. The local church leaders had been asking God for an impartation of the prophetic. As the prayer meeting continued people saw the prophetic eagle in the spirit. Those who could see said this time it was looking fearsome with a sharp beak and its wings set like a missile. He moved like a rocket up from the earth punching portholes in the thick dark cloud that brought separation from the heavens. Every time he violently punched a hole in the cloud the light would shine through.

The eagle continued to war for a few days after the team had stopped praying. The thick cloud totally cleared away. In the realm of the spirit there had been a battle to make space for this new prophetic time. Later in the week the team prayed and commissioned Robert and Sarah into their apostolic prophetic positions in the church in the Philippines. Just before the team left Sarah had a dream about God's plans and when she woke up she realized that she was covered with silver and there was silver all over her bed. God's purposes are not just revealed in words but by the power of God and signs from heavens. A mark of the apostolic ministry must be the demonstrations of the supernatural realms.

Angels in the Hills of Wales

Over a period of time three ladies in the local church saw angels working on the hills around the town. They appeared to be digging wells and making preparations—as if for the gathering of an army. At one point the angels came into the town to check it out and look it over. The area was in a time of preparation for a move of God that would be coming. I spoke to the three people individually to test out the things they were seeing and I was amazed at the consistency of the accounts and the timing. During this time I visited a conference where one of the speakers was Heidi Baker. The conference was not in our area and she did not ask me where I was from but nevertheless she prophesied about the angels that had gathered in our hills and that the heavens were opening to bring a healing revival to the region.

Revival Angels

It is now over 100 years since the Welsh revival. My hometown did not experience the revival although it came very close to the town. The following is an account of some of the things that have been seen recently in a local village, a place that had been impacted by God during the Welsh revival.

The story begins in February 2004 when Claire Dillamore and Paul Stevens went to a local village in response to a word that God had given to Paul. Paul's story follows.

I had recently read an article on the Internet about the Welsh Revival. In the article it mentioned a local village. I was thinking I should go to this village to collect some angels from there. I went there and knew that some angels came with me. I wanted to go back again.

Claire and I looked at a chapel building and I saw four angels pressed up against the windows. They were trapped and trying to get out. She was confused as to why they couldn't get out because she'd seen angels fly through closed windows before. Claire asked God why they were there and he said, "Because of the prayers of the saints." It was as if the people who had established the chapel during the revival of 100 years ago had sought to contain the blessing they had experienced. It was not out of selfishness, but they had experienced something so powerful they didn't want it to end. It was difficult to believe it could get any better.

As Claire and Paul prayed, the angels were set free and they saw them come out of the chapel. There were four different types of angel: a worship angel carrying a harp; a healing angel; an angel of

147

warfare and protection, carrying a sword; and another who was carrying a baby in his arms. This angel had a responsibility to protect local children. They commissioned the four angels as a team to go house to house through the village, starting with that street.

Before they left they looked to see what the name of the chapel was. Even before Claire found the name, she thought in her spirit it would be "Ebenezer." It took a while to find the name because it wasn't posted on any of the signs around the door. Then they saw "Ebenezer" carved into the bricks above the entrance. When Claire asked God why this was significant she found Ebenezer means *thus far has the Lord blessed us*. In this situation, it felt as if the declaration "thus far and no further" had been made and that the declaration had contained the blessing and the angels.

They drove through the village, praying as they went. As they drove past a huge chapel Claire thought, "A gathering place for angels, just like Bethlehem." They stopped and saw that the chapel was called Bethlehem! They asked God to gather the angels from all over the village. It seemed that some chapels in the village had a solitary angel watching over them. The angels were not free to leave their posts until God released them—they were isolated. Today, though, they all gathered on a patch of ground next to the chapel.

All together they were aware of 12 angels. There were at least two worship angels with instruments and one angel that was head and shoulders above the rest. He was a leader angel stationed there to coordinate the team, bring instruction and provide leadership for the others. Seeing this, Paul and Claire felt that from then on there would always be at least two angels at the gathering place. Knowing this, the angels were secure in going out and about in the village, assured that there was a place to come back to. Paul and Claire sensed that the angels would be discipled by going out and doing, then coming back and learning from their experience—like Jesus taught the disciples.

Paul got out of the car to walk around and pray. As he was doing this Claire was suddenly aware of music in the air. At first she thought it was coming from the pub nearby but it didn't sound like popular music. Then she realized she was hearing the angels worshiping.

When Paul returned, he confirmed that there had been no music coming from the pub.

During another visit to the village a few weeks later a worship angel appeared and followed Claire out of the village. This angel has made a number of appearances since. He is a revival worship angel. He suddenly appeared at a later date in one of our church meetings, and he even joined a team that traveled to India!

I was with Claire and some others the last time we saw this worship angel in Wales. We were aware that he had come with us in the car, and we were praying by the lake in Llandrindod for God to open up a healing and revival well. He left the car and started flying over the surface of the water to stir the waters. As he did so, lots of birds started flying around in the same pattern. We left him there flying over the water. We sensed he was lost in worship and having fun.

On one other visit to the local village the angels that had been left on guard after the previous visits were still there. The Holy Spirit spoke and said they were "sentinels." These angels have a watching but also a protective function. They are armed as well and stationed to protect the village.

Gathering Angels

In the same way as people have different functions and responsibilities, there are angels that carry different areas of responsibility. I was once involved in planting a new church. In the early days of the church we prophesied over every visitor. On one particular morning I was aware of a couple of angels standing at the door of the meeting room. I asked the Holy Spirit to reveal what the angels were doing. I felt they were gathering angels but I must admit I was not sure at this point. At the same time I was confident that God had spoken.

Suddenly four visitors arrived, a very significant number for our small gathering. The angels were there for a couple of weeks until I noticed they had gone. When I asked the Holy Spirit where they had gone, he said, "They are off gathering, of course."

Angels of Fire

I love the times when God, by His grace, moves in meetings in great power. I was speaking at the annual "Hungry for Him" conference. As usual the worship was great; I was pondering the things that God had given me to say. Suddenly the Holy Spirit said that I had fireballs in my hands and I was to throw them. I was not too sure about this word as this had never happened before. I kept praying and asking God to make it obvious what He was doing.

The lady leading worship suddenly said, "I see an angel of revival over the meeting and he is throwing fireballs over the people." I was amazed, and later found out this lady did not normally bring this type of word. When the time came for me to speak I knew that I had to line up with the angelic and actually throw the fireballs. I was very nervous as I picked my target for the first throw. As I threw this invisible fireball, the person was powerfully hit by God even though she had been rummaging in her bag. I threw a few others and we saw the power of God move. I knew that each time I threw a fireball the revival angel was releasing his fireball from Heaven.

A Lesson About Angels

I was praying during the worship asking God to work with me with angels and fire. I became aware of two angels standing very close to me, one on each side. It felt that if I moved to the left or right that I would flatten them over. I was also aware that there was a bank of angels gathered behind the place where I was going to preach. I do not want to express a confidence that I did not have, I just had impressions of what was going on. When I preached I was very aware of the power of God moving in an unusual way. It amused me that the angels either side of me moved as I moved. The three of us moved in perfect harmony. I asked God to confirm the things I was seeing with the eyes of my heart.

This is why I am so grateful for the seers. At the end of the meeting a woman came up to me and asked me if I was aware of the angels during the meeting. I said yes and asked her to tell me where she saw the angels. She described the two angels next to me and how they moved in tandem, even though it looked as if I would knock them over, I didn't. I was so excited and asked her where the other angels were. She described the bank of angels behind me. As soon as she left another lady came rushing up very excited about the things she saw. I did not give any clues and she explained in exactly the same manner the positioning of the angels, and how we had all moved in tandem.

Chapter 16

LEARNING TO SEE

In this chapter we look at some of the principles to help develop our ability to see in the spirit. I believe that it is part of the birthright of every believer to see in the heavenly realms. The Garden of Eden sets our expectation. I believe that God wants to take us far beyond this beginning stance. When we get to the last book in the Bible, the Book of Revelation, we find that God is still revealing new things.

If we are going to set out on the journey to learn to see in the spirit, then it will be a step of faith. We will never look if we do not believe that there is something to see. Jesus says: *"I tell you the truth, no one can see the kingdom of God unless he is born again"* (John 3:3).

Although I had very strong impressions that angels were round about, I was desperate to learn how to actually see the angels. I wanted to see the Kingdom, not just hear about it. I recognize that some people are born with a gifting to see. I have learned to see a bit more with the help of those who see clearly. Before I became a Christian I did not use my spiritual eyes at all. I was blind to spiritual things. I started from the beginning.

Recently I was watching a documentary that revealed a number of significant things that had to happen if someone was to regain their natural sight. Some of these principles are also relevant to us as we learn to use our spiritual sight. We look at this in the context of the healing of the blind man.

The disciples were in the middle of one of their many life-changing sessions with Jesus, when supernatural demonstrations were mixed with challenging teaching. The full story of the blind man regaining his sight is found in Mark chapter 8. In this passage there are a number of insights into the *process* of gaining spiritual sight before the actual miracle took place.

Prior to healing the blind man the disciples had witnessed the amazing miracle of feeding 4,000 people with only a few small fish and seven loaves. After this miracle the disciples got into a boat with Jesus and realized that they brought along only one loaf of bread. They start to talk about the lack of bread and Jesus, in His perfect teaching style challenges the disciples:

> *"Why are you talking about having no bread? Do you still not see or understand? Are your hearts hardened? Do you have eyes but fail to see, and ears but fail to hear?"* (Mark 8:17-18).

Made to See

Jesus points to different levels of *sight*. He is not talking about spiritual eyes—we have spiritual eyes but we need to see. The key to opening up our spiritual eyes to see is our hearts. If our heart is hard toward the things of God we will not see. The principle is the same for hearing and seeing. If you do not believe that God can speak today then you will find that your heart is hardened to this possibility. You will not expect to hear God speak and even if He does you will not discern His voice.

If you believe that God can speak into your life and the situations that you experience each day, then you start by positioning yourself to hear God's voice. Your heart will be soft to the voice of God. I can still remember starting to recognize the voice of God over 20 years ago. I was convinced that God wanted to speak but was not sure *how* He spoke. Over a period of time I believed God was speaking to me.

The proof came when I saw the things God had spoken to me about come to pass. I took hold of the promise of God that His sheep would know His voice.

As time went on I became more accustomed to the voice of the Spirit. It was during this time that I also learned to prophesy. I was convinced that God was able to speak and wanted to speak into every aspect of life. This gift did not depend on my knowing about subject, it depended on God knowing and revealing it through me. Most of the time God would speak to me through words, sometimes I would get pictures describing the situation.

I began to realize that the same principles that applied to prophesy also applied to seeing in the spirit. We are all made by God to see in the spiritual realms. Initially it may take a bit of time for our eyes to become accustomed to seeing. It is rather like the light being switched on in a dark room. While in the dark our eyes adjust accordingly, when the light is turned on, we don't see clearly immediately. Our eyes have to become accustomed to the new light, then we begin to see. Even when we do see, it may take a while before we understand the meaning of the things around us—to become familiar with new surroundings.

It is clear from the prophets that they often did not understand the things they saw. Just because we do not understand something should not stop us from starting the journey. The way we soften our hearts toward God in this area is by having a simple faith that He will open our eyes to the heavenly realms. We then position ourselves before God in prayer and ask the Holy Spirit to lead us into this realm of experience. There is more about this topic later.

Healing the Blind Man

A blind man from Bethsaida, was brought to Jesus by people who begged Jesus to heal him (Mark 8:22-26). The disciples had just been told they could not see, so this demonstration would be significant. Jesus took the man's hand and led him out of the city. Then Jesus spits into his eyes and lays His hands on the man. This is not conventional praying by any stretch of our imagination. He then asks the man what he can see. The man's response is surprising: *"I see people; they look like trees walking around"* (Mark 8:24).

I have heard many explanations about the man's response including one that says even Jesus could not heal everyone the first time. This explanation is simply wrong. Jesus did not have a problem raising the dead; He certainly was not going to have any difficulty opening a man's eyes. I believe that Jesus used this healing to demonstrate to His disciples some principles of the Kingdom. The fact the healing did not happen straight away must have caught the disciple's attention, it was unusual.

Jesus lays hands on the man again: *"Once more Jesus put his hands on the man's eyes. Then his eyes were opened, his sight was restored, and he saw everything clearly"* (Mark 8:25). Jesus demonstrated that there are two stages in being able to see with the eyes of the heart. One part is our eyes being opened, the second is being able to understand and interpret what we see.

Restored Sight

The documentary that I saw illustrated this process from a natural point of view. They followed the story of various people who had lost their sight for a number of years. The nature of the sight problem was such that, as medicine improved later in their lives they had an operation to restore their sight. I always thought that when their eyes were repaired everything would be straightforward and they would see. It was interesting to learn that the next stage of using their sight was not that easy.

The newly-sighted people had to re-learn how to use their eyes, and their brains had to start the process of interpreting the new vision. It was apparent that the brain did not have the ability to distinguish between different images. There are things that a fully sighted person would take for granted that take the person with newly restored sight time to process. The way these people described what they saw was very much like the man Jesus healed. Men seemed like trees walking, the images were blurred. The intense concentration that the newly-sighted person needs to see details makes them tired and often they just close their eyes again. Even though a whole new world was opened to them they did not have a reference grid.

The newly-sighted person had to learn how to judge perspective and distance—was it small in size or a long way off. When they looked out a window and saw mountains in the distance it took the brain time to interpret the picture. When they saw a bird flying across the sky and going behind a tree, the brain told the person that the bird had totally disappeared. Fully sighted people take these aspects of seeing for granted, like the ability to distinguish between men and women by looking at their features.

Learning facial features is not an easy task, for example not all men have short hair and not all women have long hair. For these newly-sighted people, the brain does not have a history of being able to distinguish between the two. What appears to be the easiest part of the process turns out to be the hardest. At the end of the documentary program it was clear that a number of people who had an operation to regain their sight never successfully made the adjustments to make full use of their new sense. They would often get depressed and tired from the over stimulation, and some people even closed their eyes and continued to live as if they had no sight.

Many of these principles also apply to us when we are learning to see into the spiritual realms. Some people will find it easier to see in the realm of the Spirit than others. Even as we start the journey to use our spiritual eyes we may not understand everything that we see. God has given us an advantage, as many things about the heavenly realms are already written in the Scriptures. He has given us information to interpret the things that we might see in the heavenly realms.

One important principle we need to learn is that just because we cannot see something doesn't mean it does not exist. This is one area where we need to take a position of maturity and faith. It is a characteristic of young children that when they close their eyes others do not exist. This thought is especially useful when they are being reprimanded! When my own children were young we would sometimes play hide and seek. Often their hiding places were not very hidden, but they thought that all they had to do was close their eyes and they would be unseen. Even if the rest of their body was poking out of the hiding place, they were always surprised when they were found. They really believed that if they could not see us then we were not there. Our starting place must be realizing that the heavenly realm exists even if we do not see it.

Where Are My Spiritual Eyes?

Some of the stories shared in the book are about angels seen by people's natural eyes—just like seeing a person. Other angels are seen with internal spiritual eyes. God has given us spiritual eyes to see. If we want to learn to see into the spiritual realm we need to know where our spiritual eyes are.

There are many ways that angels can be seen. As we look through the Scriptures we see that angels make appearances on earth. They can appear in dreams and visions. There are also times when people are caught up into the heavenly realms. Here I will focus on the eyes of our hearts and how we can discern angelic activity.

As I have learned to use my spiritual eyes I have found that I get impressions on the inside, sometimes with great detail. The evidence of their presence is then seen by the activity of God in the room. I have not seen with my natural eyes; I have seen with the eyes of my heart. It does not matter if my natural eyes are open or closed. In a story I have told elsewhere I watched an angel come behind someone speaking; I did not discern the angels with my natural eyes, although my eyes were open.

In Ephesians Paul speaks of the eyes of the heart.

> *I pray also that the eyes of your heart may be enlightened in order that you may know the hope to which he has called you, the riches of his glorious inheritance in the saints, and his incomparably great power for us who believe...* (Ephesians 1:18-19).

This passage leaves us with a question. Where are the eyes of my heart and how can I learn to use them for God's glory? If we want to open up this realm then we need to start in faith.

Later in Ephesians we get another glimpse of where our internal eye is: *Now to him who is able to do immeasurably more than all we ask or imagine, according to his power that is at work within us* (Eph. 3:20).

158

Our imagination is our internal place of seeing. Many people may struggle with this issue as they have been taught that our mind is our enemy. Bill Johnson in his book, *The Supernatural Power of the Transformed Mind,* says that the mind is the gateway to the supernatural.[1] Our imagination is a good thing, in fact God can do more than we can ever imagine. The issue is not our imagination; it is the source of the images that come into our imagination. This is why it is critical that we control what comes through our natural sight, as these things will become fuel to our imagination. If we are going to see into the realm of the spirit we need to allow the source to be our spirit. The scripture puts it this way:

> *Therefore, I urge you, brothers, in view of God's mercy, to offer your bodies as living sacrifices, holy and pleasing to God—this is your spiritual act of worship. Do not conform any longer to the pattern of this world, but be transformed by the renewing of your mind. Then you will be able to test and approve what God's will is—his good, pleasing and perfect will* (Romans 12:1-2).

When we allow our minds to be transformed to think in the way that God does, we are well on the way to engaging in fresh ways the whole realm of the angels and the supernatural.

God Gave Us Imagination

I started to recognize how God uses our imagination through the operation of the prophetic gift. One of the exercises I use when training people to see is to get every person to pray for someone in their group and ask God to give them a picture. The battle people always have is whether the picture is from God or from their own thinking. As we do this in a safe practice environment, people are able to share their picture and see if it is relevant to the other person. I remember one of the first times I used this exercise. I had a picture of a brand new extension looking out from the back of a house. The house itself still looked like it needed some restoration. I shared the picture with the person, who told me that their house was in the process of being restored and they had been considering adding an extension on the back of the house. They were not sure if it was the right way to spend money. The picture was confirmed and I knew that the origin had been the Spirit.

The same principle is true when learning to see into the spiritual realm. We have to put ourselves in a place of dependence on God and ask Him to show us what is going on around us. We are told that the Word of God is confirmed by two or more witnesses. I am privileged to know a number of people who see easily. I always check out what they are seeing, in this way I learn quickly when it is something that God is showing me.

One day I was driving past the church building in the middle of the week. I could see with my inner eye a couple of angels sitting on top of the roof as if they were just hanging around waiting for some action. I had not realized at that time that angels can be a bit like teenagers! The next day I was speaking to a lady in the church and suddenly she said that I would probably think she was mad but as she was driving past the building she saw some angels waiting around. She then told me that when the church gathered they would go and collect other angels to come to the meeting.

I realized that often God allows our eyes to be open to see things so that when we come to times that are more critical we will have a confidence in what He is doing. There have been times when the church has gathered together and an angel has come into the room. I have been totally unaware of the angel's presence but have obeyed the prompting of the Holy Spirit to pray for people in a certain way or even in a certain place. At the end of the meetings I have been told how the things that I did were working with the angels in the room.

In one meeting someone told me they had been watching chariots of fire moving in a meeting, my wife started to pray that God would release His fire in the meeting. In the same gathering someone saw small angels lying on the lap of a large angel. This mirrored exactly the position of a little boy on his daddy's lap—a visible illustration of God's presence at the meeting.

Getting Started

My greatest desire for you is that you will begin to see what God has for you to experience. Some of you will have a strong ability to see and this book will have confirmed what is already going on. For others the journey is only just beginning. Here are a few pointers to help you along the way.

Seek and You Will Find

I tell you the truth, anyone who has faith in me will do what I have been doing. He will do even greater things than these, because I am going to the Father. And I will do whatever you ask in my name, so that the Son may bring glory to the Father. You may ask me for anything in my name, and I will do it (John 14:12-14).

As a parent there are many things that I want my children to enjoy, but it is important that they learn to ask! Our heavenly Father likes us to ask Him for things. As we ask, and keep asking, our heavenly Father to open the eyes of our hearts and teach us to see, it is a prayer that He delights to answer. It is through prayer that we engage our faith to a place of action. He is able to do more than we could ever ask or imagine.

Working Together

The best place to learn to see with the eyes of your heart is with other people. This way you are able to test and receive confirmation about the things you are seeing. We were born into a family, and God wants us to learn and grow as His family. If we try and grow in isolation then our growth will be slower and we could even be in danger of walking into error.

Practice

In the Book of Hebrews we are told that we learn to distinguish between good and evil through practice. If you follow any professional sport you will realize that the players spend more time in training than they do in a game. The thing about the training sessions is the players have every opportunity to improve their skills without the fear of making mistakes.

None of us like making mistakes, the Church needs to have places where believers can practice moving in all the supernatural gifts. Some of the best times I have had in learning to see in the Spirit and to hear the voice of Spirit is when we have told each other we are practicing! During these times we can say what we see as God sharpens us and we gain a confidence in the Holy Spirit. I have been in wonderful meetings when we have shared together the things we are seeing. As we shared we found the heart of God and worked with the angelic realm and saw the power of God released in many ways.

Don't Give Up

It is so easy to give up, especially if there is no one to bring us encouragement. In the Bible, Timothy is told to stir up the gift of God that is in him by the laying on of hands. (See 2 Timothy 1:6.) We have the gift of God in us to see in the Spirit. There will be many times when we need to stir up the gift that is within us. This means that we put ourselves on the inside—in a place of action. Do not be discouraged because we feel we are not getting very far or there are other people around us who do not understand.

Write Things Down

It is too easy to forget things that God has shown us. When God shows you things, you may find it beneficial to write them down. Having a journal will also help you stay accurate about the things that God has shown you. Many of the details that I have shared in this book have been possible because people had taken the time to write about their experiences. I am sure there are many exciting spiritual events that have been forgotten because they were never put to paper. When I write I will put everything down, even if later I realize that some things were from my own heart and not from God.

Tuning in the Picture

When you start seeing in the Spirit things may not be very clear and you may be uncertain if they are from God. In the past when we bought a new television we had to take time to tune it so we could get a good, clear picture. Sometimes we even had to adjust the receiving antennae. The same is true with things of the Spirit. At first I might be unsure if I have have the right channel, but over time I become familiar with the type of programs that I see on that particular channel. My children can tell just by looking which channel has their favorite programs coming up. As we learn to see in the Spirit we will become familiar with things, even if the things that God is showing us are new.

Angels and Demons

As the eyes of your heart become more familiar with the spiritual realm then you will discern both angelic and demonic activity. I always say that a demon is like a spider, it just needs to be removed and not feared. We have been given greater authority in Christ than any demon.

Ask Questions

Have you noticed that little children have the ability to ask questions all day long? If they do not understand something, they will simply ask another question. After we think we are grown up we think we know everything so we stop asking questions and spend our time sharing our knowledge. A new Christian recently told me that I would probably get tired of him asking questions. On the contrary, I hope he never stops asking. Not only does the one questioning grow, but I grow as well. Whether you are learning to see or have become mature in God, keep asking questions of Him and questions of other people. That way you will keep on growing.

I love the dialogue in the Book of Zechariah. An angel comes to Zechariah, a prophet, wakes him up and asks him what he sees. Having answered him, Zechariah then says:

> *I asked the angel who talked with me, "What are these, my lord?"*
> *He answered, "Do you not know what these are?" "No, my lord," I*
> *replied. So he said to me, "This is the word of the Lord to Zerubba-*
> *bel: 'Not by might nor by power, but by My Spirit,' says the Lord*
> *Almighty" (Zechariah 4:4-6).*

The amazing revelation came as a result of asking questions. I have found many times when God has spoken or shown me things that the depth of revelation comes when I have asked more questions.

When you see something in the Spirit, ask God what you are seeing. Ask Him what He is doing, what His angels are doing. The angels have different jobs and you can understand how to partner with them to see the supernatural manifest on earth.

Enjoy the Journey

There are many realms of Heaven to be uncovered. Just think about the natural world for a moment. How many countries are there, people groups, animals, plants, birds, weather conditions—how much knowledge is there about His creation on earth? In the same way there is so much to discover about the earth, there is even more to find out about the heavenly realms.

Try not to limit yourself by other people's experiences. Ask God to take you off the map and enjoy greater adventures and blessings.

Endnote

1. Johnson, Bill. *The Supernatural Power of the Transformed Mind* (Shippensburg, PA: Destiny Image Publishers, 2005).

Chapter 17

GO WITH WHAT
YOU HAVE

Go with what you have, it will be more than you think. Peter was going to the place of prayer when he was asked for money. He responded:

"Silver or gold I do not have, but what I have I give you. In the name of Jesus Christ of Nazareth, walk." Taking him by the right hand, he helped him up, and instantly the man's feet and ankles became strong. He jumped to his feet and began to walk... (Acts 3:6-8).

He understood what he had. The result was an amazing miracle in the name of Jesus. I made a decision to be like Abraham, to saddle my donkey and go on a journey. It is possible to start out on a journey at any time, but there are times when it is easier to make the journey. I am writing this after a few days of snow. The British do not generally fair so well when the snow falls and things come to a standstill. One person said that he normally had a 30 minute journey to work which in the snow took him over two and a half hours.

We are in a time of acceleration of God's purposes and the release of the supernatural in the whole body of Christ. The snow is melting and the journey will be easier and quicker than in the past! This is not about specialists, it is for us all. We should have a higher expectation of supernatural events, healings, and angelic visitations in the months and years to come. We are in a time of many changes in the spiritual climate. Many prophets have been speaking of increase in the apostolic ministry that will affect the Church and business.

These advances of God's purposes on earth are reflected by an increased activity in the angelic realm. Apostles are earthly messengers and angels are heavenly messengers. The apostolic responsibility is to be messengers of the Gospel and to serve and prepare the Church so it engages the fullness of her destiny and purpose.

> *It was he who gave some to be apostles, some to be prophets, some to be evangelists, and some to be pastors and teachers, to prepare God's people for works of service, so that the body of Christ may be built up until we all reach unity in the faith and in the knowledge of the Son of God and become mature, attaining to the whole measure of the fullness of Christ* (Ephesians 4:11-13).

The full releasing of this foundational gifting on earth only came through the death and the resurrection of the ultimate apostle Jesus Christ Himself. The mark of any genuine apostolic ministry is to serve the Body of Christ, in the process modeling the very attitude of Christ who made Himself nothing that the Church could become something—the effective sons of God. The angels are released to serve the sons through Christ.

As we move forward in this time of restoration, we will see a rapid return to the power of the New Testament Church that had the ability to turn cities upside down. I am convinced that we will see far beyond this. The apostolic ministry should be surrounded by signs and wonders, part of this change will be a dramatic increase in angelic activity in the Church. Everything we have looked at belongs to the whole Church. If we are willing to go off our map we will find that we are on God's map of the supernatural. God does not need to act when we can, but He will act when we can't.

At this time God is looking for those who will become the doorways to growth in the supernatural. Will you be one of those people? The opportunity is for anyone who will answer the call. The atmosphere for the supernatural and angelic visitations is open to everyone who will believe and engage with God. The responsibility of those who see clearly is to train others to see as well. The fresh partnership with the heavenly realms will release a new sound from the Church as it only does what it sees the Father doing. The miracles will come at an increasing level; creative miracles will be seen. The angels of death will be defeated by the angels of life as resurrections become normal.

I would love to say that these things will happen automatically, but I do not believe that God has planned it that way. A number of years ago I had a dream that spoke to me clearly about what I needed to do. In the dream the meeting I was attending had finished even though I felt I had to give a tongue and interpretation inspired by the Spirit. As everyone left to get their tea and coffee I went to the other side of the room away from the crowd and started to bring the tongue.

The congregation soon regathered as I acted out the interpretation. I started to lean to the left as I gave the tongue. In the dream I continued to lean until I was almost horizontal. It would have been an impossible position to hold in real life. The Holy Spirit was saying: will you lean on me? Then I realized I could take my feet off the ground. I did not do so as I was frightened people would think I was levitating. I knew that, through the dream, God was asking if I would trust Him to the point when I was totally dependent on Him.

Will you trust Him on the journey? If you do, the angels will come and meet you and take you off your map to the glorious realms beyond. Salvation and healing will be part of your inheritance.